MURDEROUS MATHS.

KAKURO
AND OTHER FIENDISH
NUMBER PUZZLES

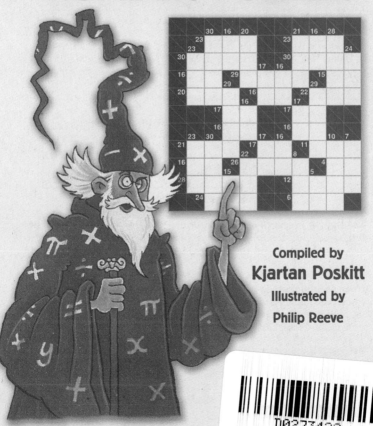

Compiled by
Kjartan Poskitt

Illustrated by
Philip Reeve

To my granny Margaret Fenton age 100. If this was a book of crossword puzzles, she'd finish it in 20 minutes.

Scholastic Children's Books,
Euston House, 24 Eversholt Street,
London NW1 1DB, UK

A division of Scholastic Ltd
London ~ New York ~ Toronto ~ Sydney ~ Auckland
Mexico City ~ New Delhi ~ Hong Kong

Published in the UK by Scholastic Ltd, 2006

10 digit ISBN 0 439 95164 X
13 digit ISBN 978 0439 95164 7

Printed and bound by Nørhaven Paperback A/S, Denmark

2 4 6 8 10 9 7 5 3 1

CONTENTS

Introduction

A few weeks ago the headquarters of the Murderous Maths Organisation was a scary place to be. It was long past midnight and all was deathly quiet and so you'd be forgiven for thinking that the place was empty, but it wasn't! All the lights were shining bright and everybody was frantically scribbling away on anything they could find including scraps of paper, old £5 notes, pizza boxes ... they were even scribbling on the pizzas themselves, but why?

The answer was SU DOKU puzzles. The MM organisation had already produced their own highly-acclaimed-international-best-selling-exquisitely-detailed-lavishly-produced-no-pages-missing-reasonably-priced-handy-for-the-bathroom Su Doku book, but in doing so the puzzles had completely taken over everybody's brains. Everyone in the organisation from the grand editor right down to the lowly rubber plant waterer was sitting in deadly silence trying to fit numbers into Su Doku grids, and covering the place with little notes and plans to help them. But as soon as one grid was completed and defeated, two more would rise up and take its place. As everyone battled valiantly to overcome the never ending* swarm of Su Dokus, the telephones went unanswered, tea was left undrunk, the grand editor's nails were unpainted, the rubber plant was unwatered and the entire might of the MM Organisation ground to a halt.

It seemed that nothing could break the addictive curse of the Su Doku until one morning a different puzzle arrived. It was to be the saviour of the MM organisation and it might even save the world as we know it.

The new puzzle was KAKURO. It's a bit like Su Doku because you fill numbers into a grid, but the difference is that as well as exercising your logic skills, you can use use your arithmetic skills too. There's just one danger with Kakuros. They are such huge fun that we're a bit worried the entire world might end up doing them instead. So although we're going to give you a load of cool Kakuros to try in this book, you'll also find there's some other puzzles too. And, of course, just in case you're getting withdrawal symptoms, we've put in a few Su Dokus just for old times' sake.

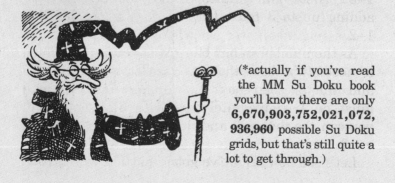

(*actually if you've read the MM Su Doku book you'll know there are only **6,670,903,752,021,072, 936,960** possible Su Doku grids, but that's still quite a lot to get through.)

Kakuro

Here's a very simple Kakuro puzzle. The idea is to fill every empty box with a digit between 1-9.

If you look at the square marked $_4\backslash^9$ this means that the digits in the boxes underneath it must add up to 4. *These digits have to be different.*

Also the digits in the boxes to the right must add up to 9, and they must be different too. The other numbered boxes also indicate what their rows and columns must add up to.

Here's the puzzle again, but we'll plonk in a few letters to make it easier to describe what we're talking about.

We know boxes a+b= 4. We also know that b+e = 3.

Here's where the clever bit starts. If you have two digits that add up to 4 *and they have to be different,* then the digits must be 1+3. Also two digits adding up to 3 must be 1+2.

As the number in box b is needed for both the 3 and the 4, then box b must be 1. Immediately you can see that a=3 and e = 2.

Let's see how far we've got:

Now look at the 8, which is telling you that $3 + d + g = 8$.

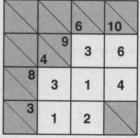

There are two ways to make 8 from three different digits: 1+2+5 or 1+3+4. However we already have a 3 in place, so the digits for d and g must be 1 and 4, but which is which?

Look at the number 6 on the top row. It's telling us that $c + d + 2 = 6$. However if d was 4 then c would have to be 0 which is not allowed. Therefore $d = 1$ and that means $c = 3$. Nearly finished! There's just boxes f and g left to fill in, and by now the answers should be obvious:

(If these last answers are *not* obvious to you, don't worry. Just abandon all hope of ever doing Kakuros and instead use this as a colouring book. There's no shame in it, in fact a lot of people who are addicted to Kakuros wish they'd just stuck to colouring in the first place.)

TRICKS

THE EXTRA BOX

Here's part of a bigger puzzle. Without filling in any other numbers, you can tell what should go in box "a"!

Look at the three numbers 12, 6 and 8 on the top. They tell us that all the boxes marked x together add up to 12+6+8 = 26.

Now if you look at the rows going across, all the boxes marked x PLUS the box marked a = 10+11+12 = 33. As 33 is 7 more than 26, this means a=7.

WHICH IS WHICH

Here's another bit of a puzzle. You can tell what x is without solving a,b,c or d!

Here you can see that a+b=3 so a must be either 1 or 2. In the same way c+d=3 so c has to be 1 or 2 as well. But as a and c are in the same row, they can't be the same so one of them is 1 and the other is 2. We don't know which is which but what we do know is that a+c=3. Therefore the 9 tells us that x has to be 6.

ONLY OPTION

Remember that you can only fill the digits 1-9 into the boxes, so can you tell what must go in box q ?

There are two ways to make 15 with two digits: 7+8 and 9+6. There are three ways to make 9 with three digits but none of them use 7,8 or 9. Therefore q must be 6.

HELPFUL NUMBERS

Some numbers make life easier. Suppose you have a row of three empty boxes with 7 at the end. The three numbers have to be 1+2+4, so 7 is helpful. However if your three boxes have 9 at the end, the numbers could be 1+3+5 or 2+3+4 or 1+2+6, so 9 is not so helpful. (Of course if you find one of the boxes has a 4 in it, then you know that the other two boxes have 2 and 3.) Here's a list of all the helpful numbers.

You'll see that the helpful numbers are only helpful with the right number of empty boxes. Although 29 is helpful with four empty boxes, if there are five empty boxes then there are *eight* different combinations that could go in! For instance 3+4+6+7+9 or 2+4+6+8+9 or 3+5+6+7+8 etc.

Number of empty boxes	Helpful number	Only possible digits
2	**3**	$1 + 2$
	4	$1 + 3$
	16	$7 + 9$
	17	$8 + 9$
3	**6**	$1 + 2 + 3$
	7	$1 + 2 + 4$
	23	$6 + 8 + 9$
	24	$7 + 8 + 9$
4	**10**	$1 + 2 + 3 + 4$
	11	$1 + 2 + 3 + 5$
	29	$5 + 7 + 8 + 9$
	30	$6 + 7 + 8 + 9$
5	**15**	$1 + 2 + 3 + 4 + 5$
	16	$1 + 2 + 3 + 4 + 6$
	34	$4 + 6 + 7 + 8 + 9$
	35	$5 + 6 + 7 + 8 + 9$

OUR EXPERT, TRUFFLES, WILL GIVE YOU A FEW TIPS TO GET STARTED. GOOD LUCK!

Dead Simple Puzzles

1

The first set of three boxes lying along the bottom line add up to 7 so they must contain 1,2 and 4. You cannot put 4 or 2 directly underneath the 4, therefore the box under the 4 must be 1. You can use this same trick SIX more times around the edges of this puzzle! Also you should be able to see that the top left corner and bottom right corner both have to be 9! Always look out for corners where the pairs of boxes add to 16 and 17.

2

The first empty box on the bottom line must be 1,
it's just like the example on page 7.
Always look out for these corners
where the pairs of boxes add to 3 and
4. This puzzle has FOUR more of
them! The 34 on the right-hand edge
is helpful, the digits must be 4,6,7,8,9.
The top digit must be the 4 as this
is the only digit you can use to add
up to the 7.

3

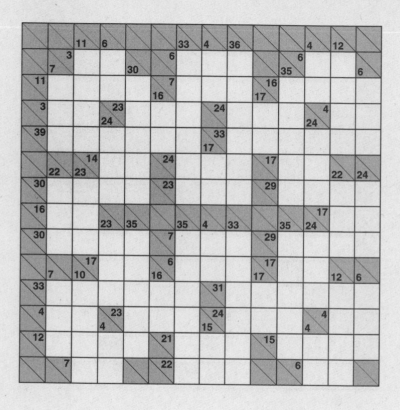

You can use the same tip I gave you for puzzle 1 three times in this puzzle. And by the way, 39 with six empty boxes is helpful! the numbers have to be 4+5+6+7+8+9.

14

4

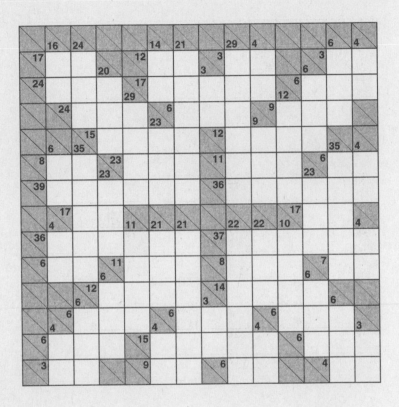

Both 21 and 22 with six empty boxes are helpful. 21= 1+2+3+4+5+6 and 22 = 1+2+3+4+5+7

5

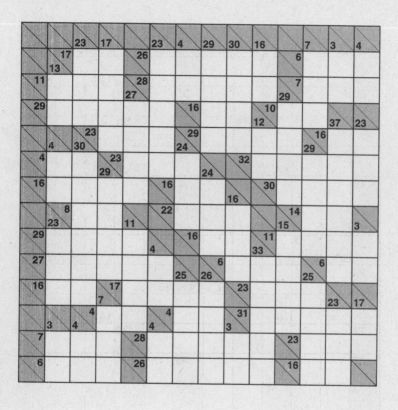

Don't forget that 29 with four empty boxes is helpful: 9+8+7+5. There are six of them here.

6

▨	↓28	↓22	▨	↓14	↓30	▨	↓29	↓13	▨	↓28	↓22
→4			→16 ↓14			→16			→4 ↓14		
→35						→35 ↓14					
→23				→22				→23			
→3			↓10	→24 ↓11				↓13	→3 ↓11		
→16					↓6	▨	→21 ↓4				
▨	▨	→6				→7				▨	▨
▨	↓26	→7 ↓28				→6				↓26	↓28
→22					↓29	↓14	→18 ↓28				
→3			↓14	→22				▨	→3 ↓14		
→24				→23 ↓16				→24 ↓16			
→35						→35					
→4			→17			→17			→4		

7

8

9

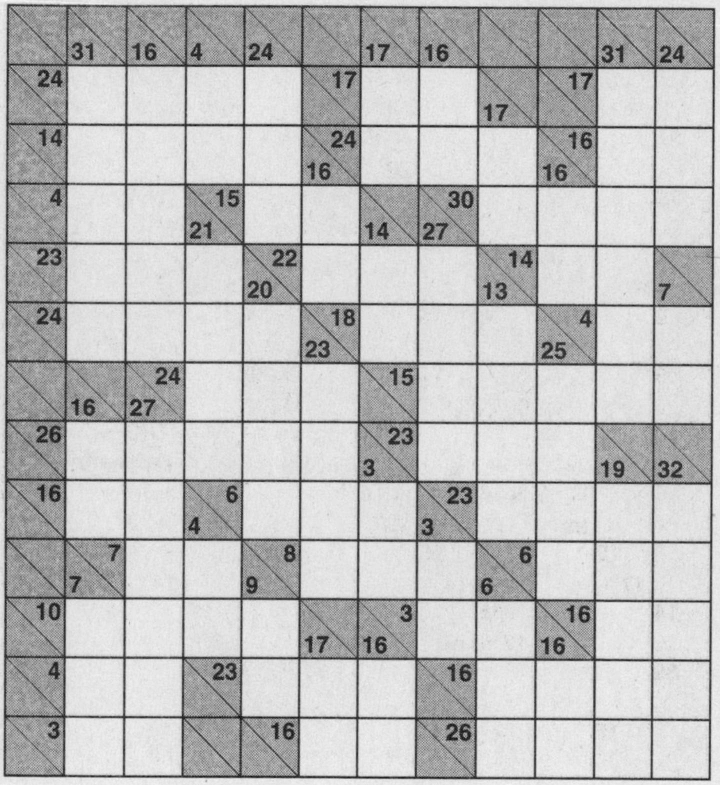
31 16 4 24 17 16 31 24
24 17 17 17
14 24 16 16 16
4 15 21 14 30 27
23 22 20 14 13 7
24 18 23 4 25
16 24 27 15
26 23 3 19 32
16 6 4 23 3
7 7 8 9 6 6
10 17 3 16 16 16
4 23 16
3 16 26

10

\	\	24\	19\	18\	\	13\	26\	\	16\	29\	\
\	14\18				\17			14\16			16\
\21					28\39						
\19						38\16			16\14		
\	6\	7\35						3\16			\
\9				\16			\4			6\	7\
\3			6\	3\17			13\10				
\10					\11			\	27\3		
\	\	29\3			25\4			22\7			
\	17\10			14\15						7\	4\
\14			17\16			13\30					
\39							\19				
\	\17			\17			\12				\

11

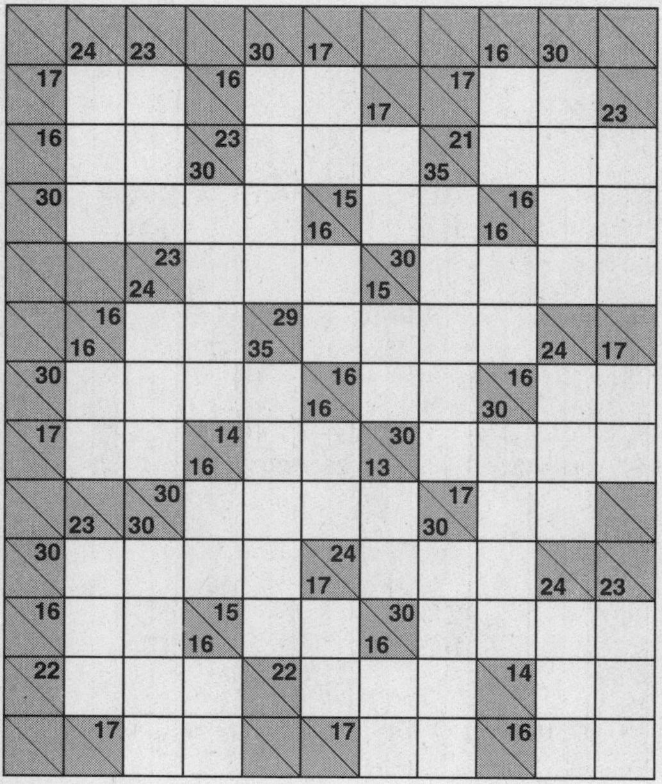
24 23 30 17 16 30
17 16 17 17 23
16 23 30 21 35
30 15 16 16 16
23 24 30 15
16 16 29 35 24 17
30 16 16 16 30
17 14 16 30 13
23 30 30 17 30
30 24 17 24 23
16 15 16 30 16
22 22 14
17 17 16

12

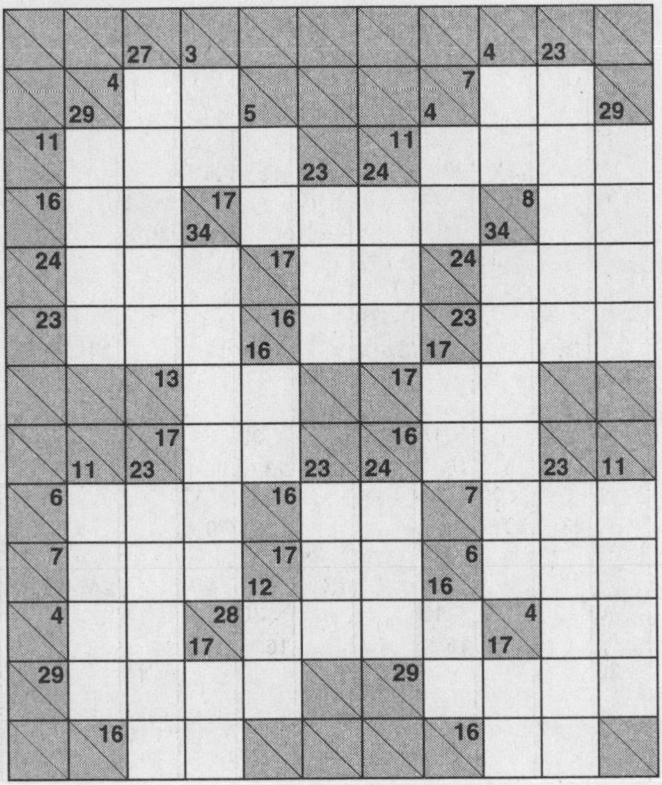

13

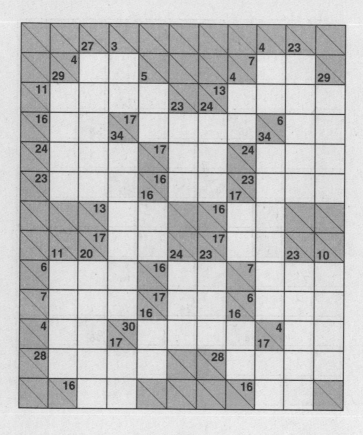

Watch out! This is very similar to puzzle 12, so you'll have to concentrate not to get mixed up!

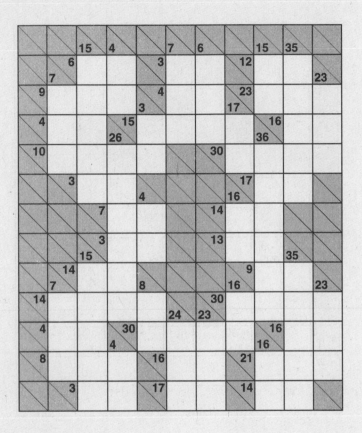

15

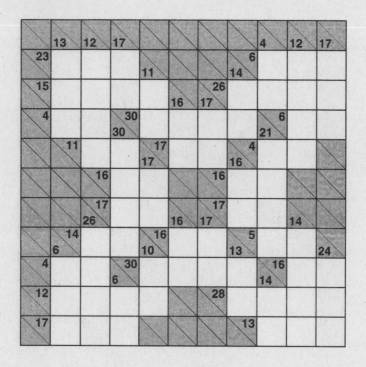

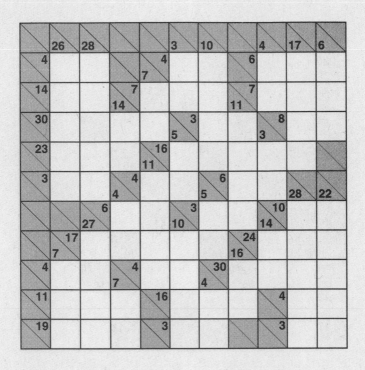

17

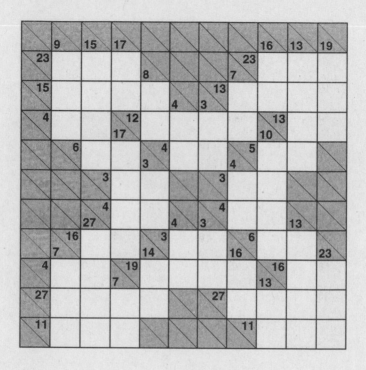

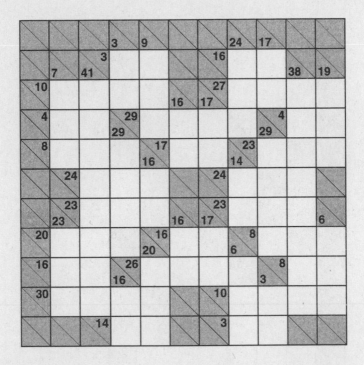

Any row of eight empty boxes is helpful! 41 uses the numbers 1,2,3,5,6,7,8,9 and 38 uses the numbers 1,2,3,4,5,6,8,9. (Subtract the number you're trying to make from 45 to find the digit you don't need. E.g. 45-41=4. This means to make 41 from 8 digits you use all the digits 1-9 except 4.)

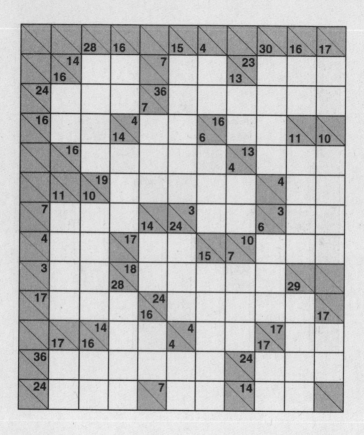

20

Devious Puzzles

21

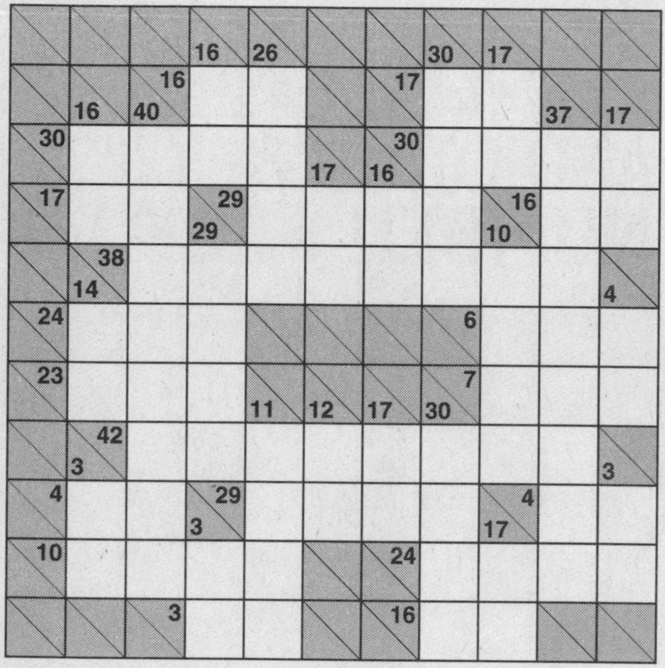

Here's an easy start to our Devious section! Remember to look out for corners where the pairs of boxes add to 16 and 17. Don't forget that 30 with four empty boxes is helpful: 9+8+7+6. Also 40, 42, 37 and 38 with 8 empty boxes are all helpful!

22

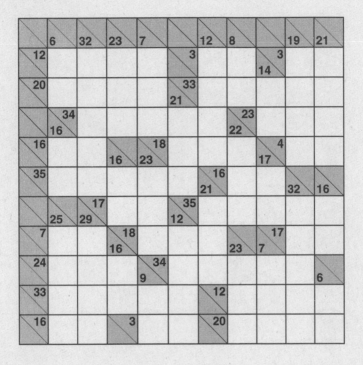

23

24

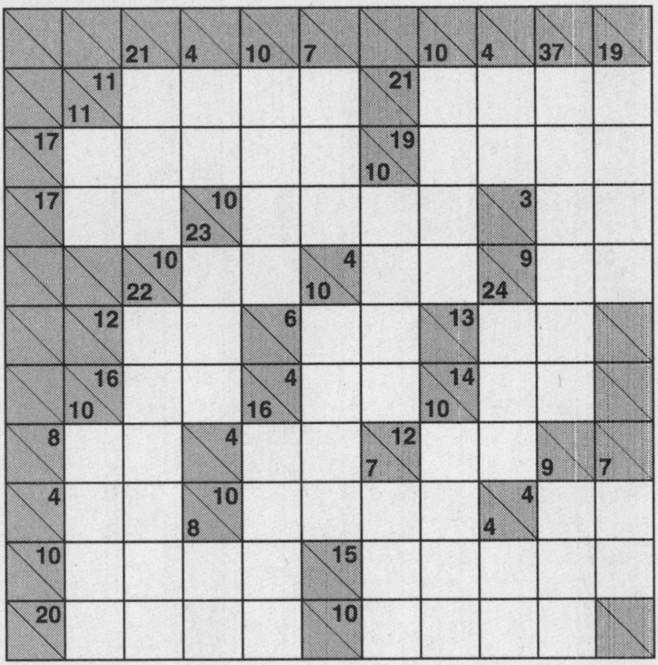

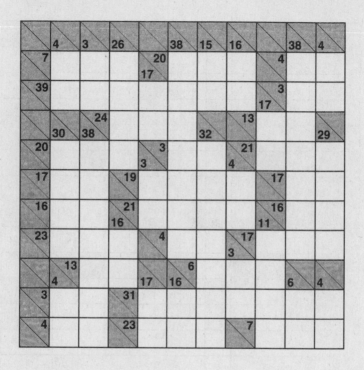

26

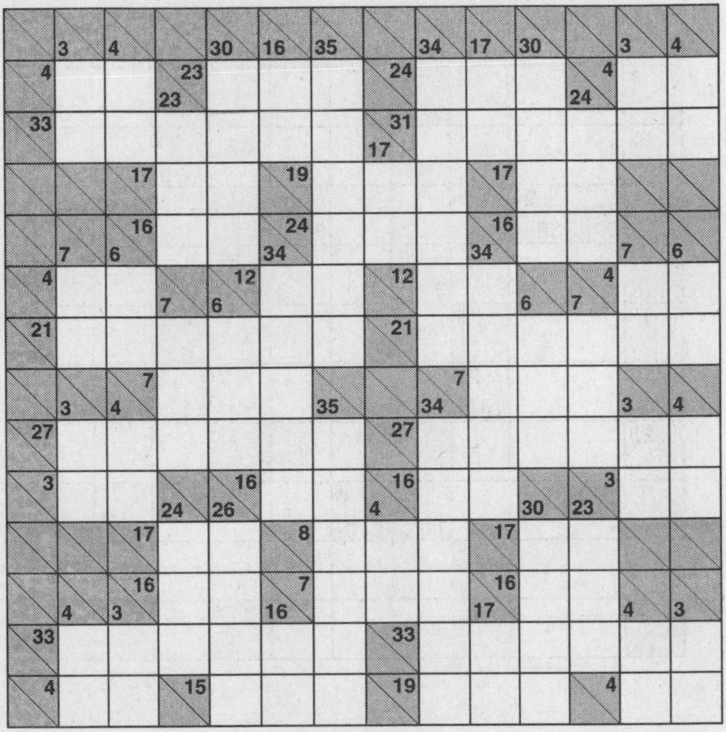
3 4 30 16 35 34 17 30 3 4
4 23 23 24 4 24
33 31 17
17 19 17
16 7 6 24 34 16 34 7 6
4 12 7 6 12 4 6 7
21 21
7 3 4 35 7 34 3 4
27 27
3 16 24 26 16 4 3 30 23
17 8 17
16 4 3 7 16 16 17 4 3
33 33
4 15 19 4

	17	11		23	16		24	16			7	13	28
16			14 / 24			17				18 / 29			
33						16			20 / 23				
19				16 / 6				23					
	23	10 / 30					32	13			12 / 21		
19			6 / 17					19 / 16				30	
16		12 / 24			17 / 17					17 / 15			23
30				24				30 / 22					
	17		11	16 / 6			16 / 24			16 / 20			
	27	14 / 12			22				23 / 17				
8		5 / 23			30 / 24						13	19	
22				15 / 17			21 / 4						
26				17			17						
12					16		6			4			

28

30

Drastic Puzzles

31

32

33

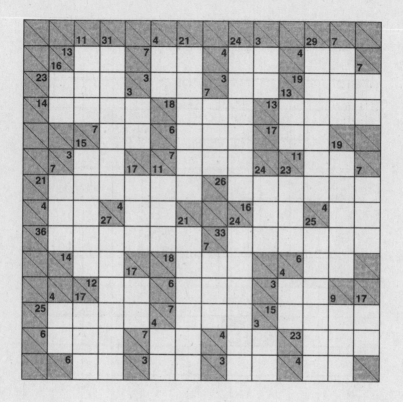

34

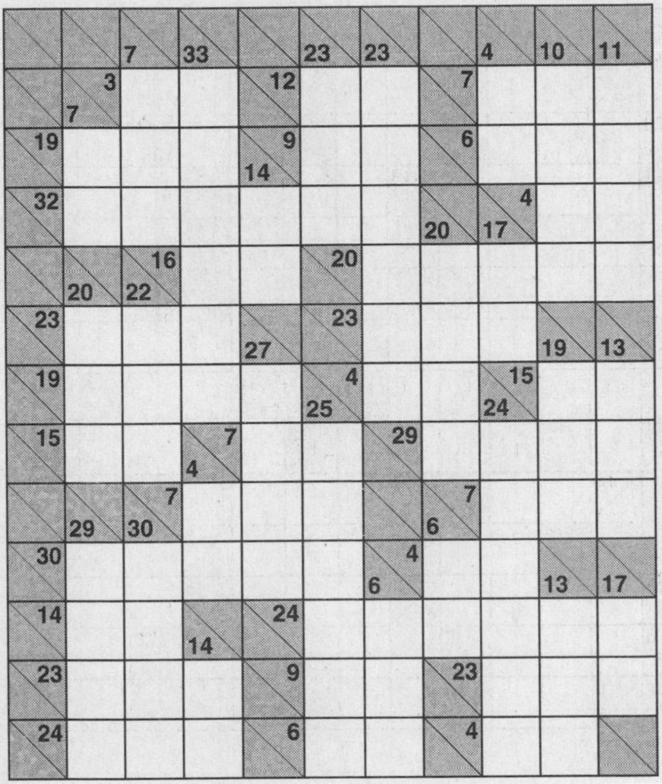

35

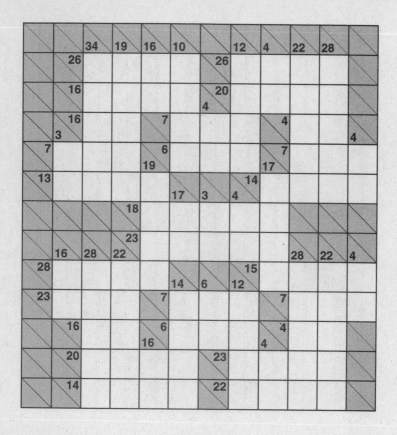

36

■	15\	14\	4\	22\	■	7\	11\	■	■	■
\11					\3			4\	28\	7\
\10					20\15					
\4			\16			16\11				
\16			14\22					14\4		
■	12\	28\13					\16			12\
\24						20\	22\9			
\9				■	16\24					
■	7\16			29\13					10\	11\
\4			4\28					\8		
\13					10\16			4\4		
\15						\10				
■	■	■	\16			\11				

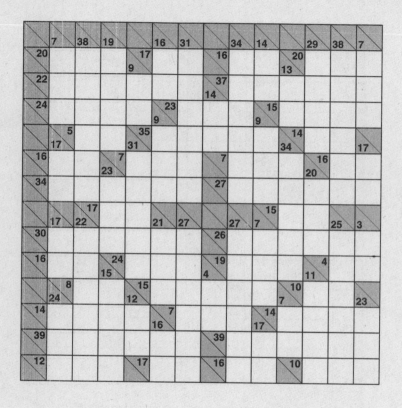

38

39

\	26\	16\	23\	\	\	\	\	7\	24\	34\
\23				21\	\	\	19\7			
\13					\	\26				
\21					16\	17\27				
\11			26\29					26\10		
\18				17\17			16\11			
\	\	\16			\	\16			\	\
\	24\	34\17			16\	17\17			34\	24\
\11				10\16			9\17			
\10			7\22					7\9		
\19					\	\19				
\27					\	\27				
\7				\	\	\	\7			

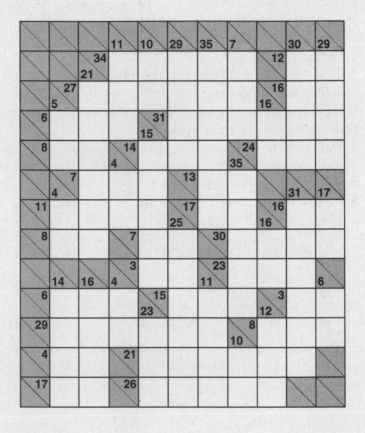

Bridges

This puzzle is perfect for arty people because you don't have to put numbers in, you just draw straight lines.

The idea is to link all the numbered islands together using bridges:
- The bridges must go horizontally or vertically and they cannot cross each other
- You can't have more than two bridges joining the same two islands. The number on each island says how many bridges must lead to it.
- All the islands must be linked up together.

Here's a VERY easy start!

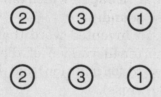

You need to link up these six islands with the right number of bridges going to each island. But you can't do this...

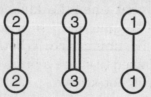

... because you can't put more than two bridges between two islands. You can't do this either...

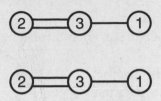

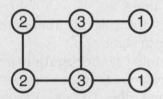

...because the two groups of islands are separate. Here is the only possible answer:

Where do the names "Kakuro" "Su Doku" and "Bridge" come from?

Logic puzzles like Kakuro and Su Doku are especially popular in Japan which is why the names have a Japanese sound.

KAKURO is an invented word that means cross sums. It's a shortened version of the words kasan (the Japanese word for addition) and kurosu (which sounds a bit like cross).

SU DOKU is short for the "Suji wa dokushin ni kagiru" which is Japanese for "the numbers must be single".

The odd bit is that when the Japanese say "single" they also mean "unmarried", so it means that the numbers must be unmarried. Whether or not the numbers are allowed to share a pizza or go out to see a band together is not known.

Incidentally the name for the BRIDGE puzzles comes from the English word "bridge" which means a bridge.

Now we'll experiment with a full puzzle and pick up a few tips.

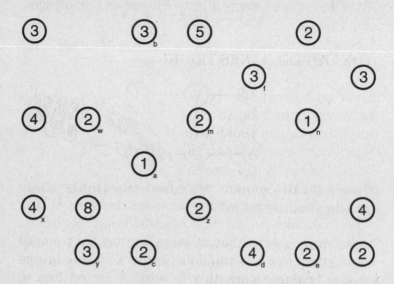

(The letters don't appear on normal puzzles, these are just for our explanations.)

The first thing to spot is the island with the number 8. This has to have two bridges going off in every direction, so we can draw two bridges going from this island to each of the islands marked w, x, y and z.

Now look at the island marked 1a. As the bridges have to be vertical or horizontal, 1a could only have been linked to island 3b or 2c but the island marked 2c is now blocked by the bridges between (8) and 2z. Therefore 1a must link with a single bridge to 3b.

So far these links are obvious and you can immediately tell if you have to put in one or two bridges. When things get tougher, sometimes it's important just to find out which islands are linked, even if you don't know if it's with one or two bridges. Try this:

THE DOTTED LINES TRICK!

Look at island 4d. It is between 2c and 2e, so you might think you could just link with two bridges to both of them. But if you do  that, you can't join any more bridges onto the group and so these three would be separate from all the other islands. As all the islands must be linked together, it means that at least one bridge from 4d must go up to 3f. As you don't know if it's one bridge or two bridges, mark this in with a dotted line to remind you to check later. This dotted line will also tell you that there cannot be a bridge between 2m and 1n.

It's always worth looking for islands with high numbers. If an island has 7 or 8 on it, then it must connect to the islands in all four directions. If an island is at the edge of the puzzle with 5 or 6 on it, then it must connect with at least one bridge in each of the three available directions. (For example, look at the island numbered 5 in our test puzzle. It has to have bridges going left, right and downwards.)

Can you complete our starting puzzle? The answer is at the end of the book.

Dead Simple Puzzles

1

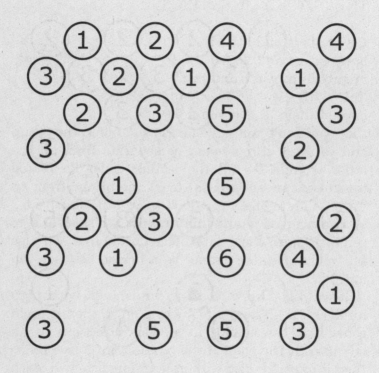

On the second row down, the two (1) islands cannot be linked or they will be isolated. Each island only has one other island it can link to, so you can draw the bridges in! Now the (2) on the second row cannot link to the (1) directly below it or the three islands will be isolated, therefore the (2) must link to the (3) at the end. On you go...

TRUFFLES' TIPS

2

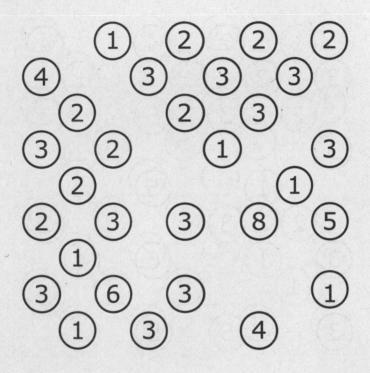

Start by filling in all eight bridges from the (8) island, and also all six bridges from the (6) island!

3

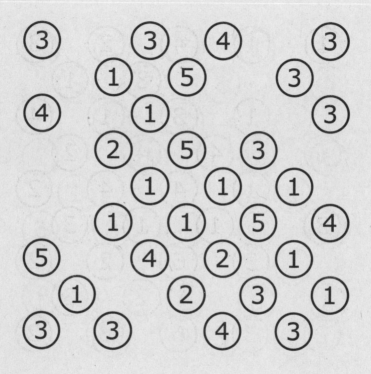

TRUFFLES' TIPS

58

4

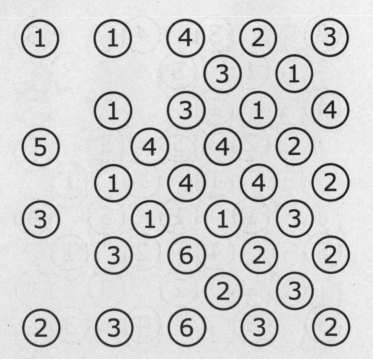

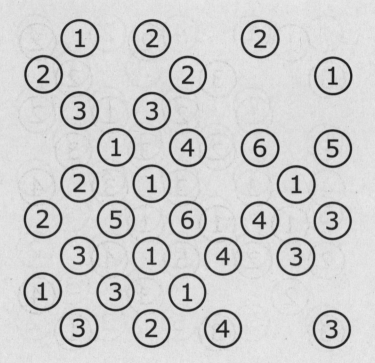

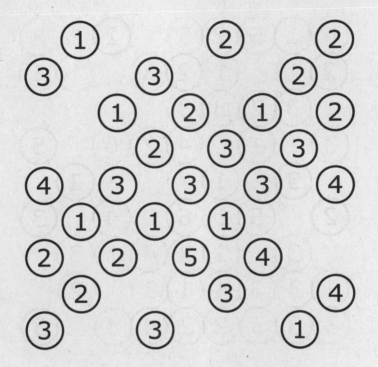

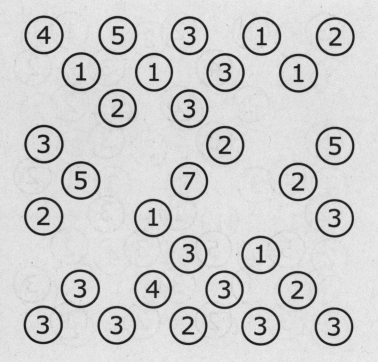

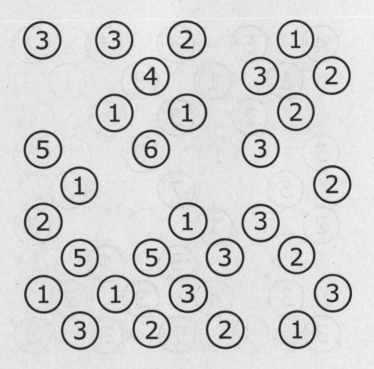

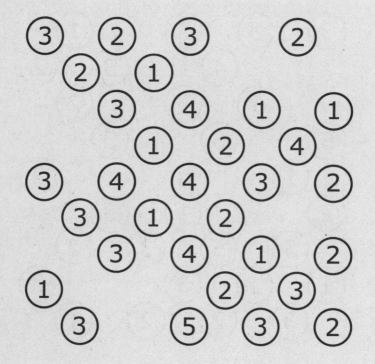

10

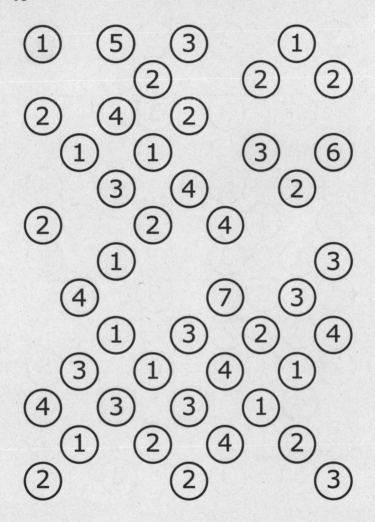

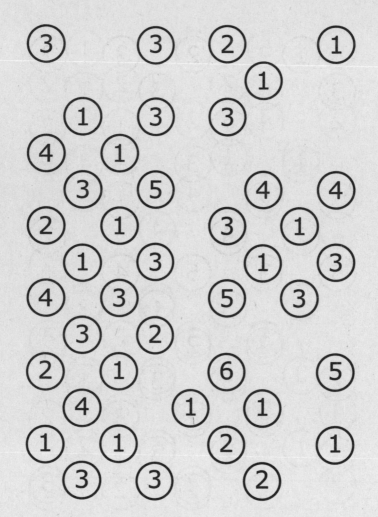

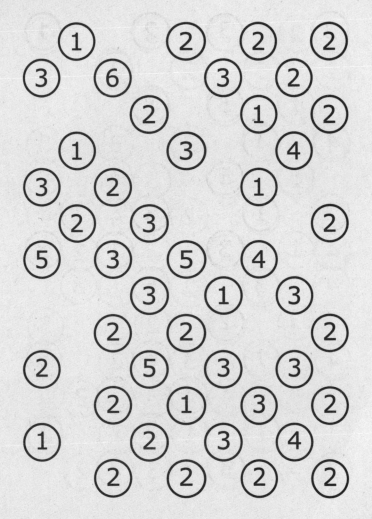

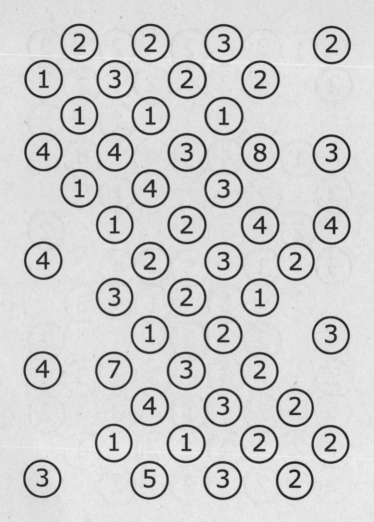

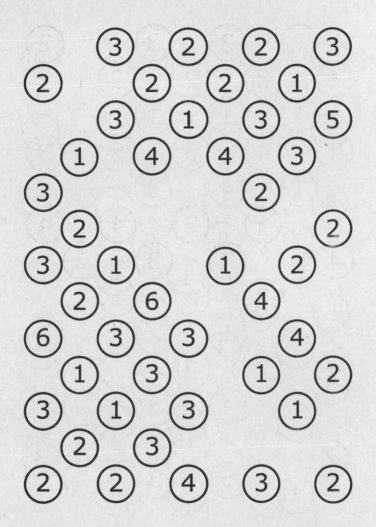

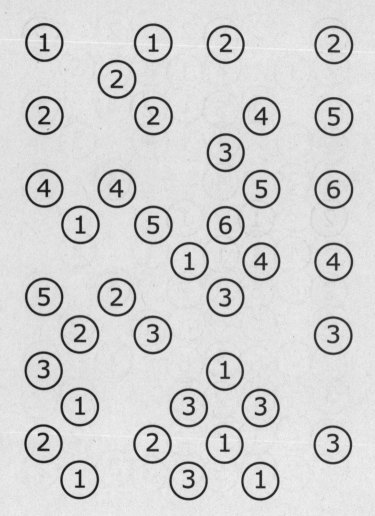

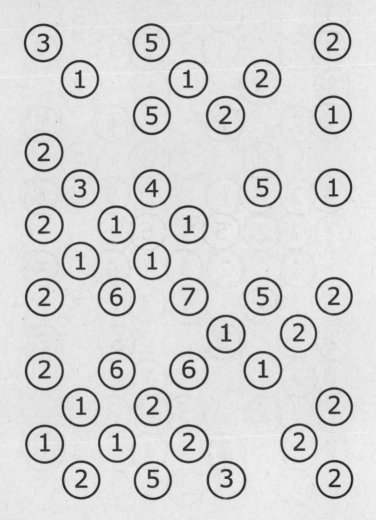

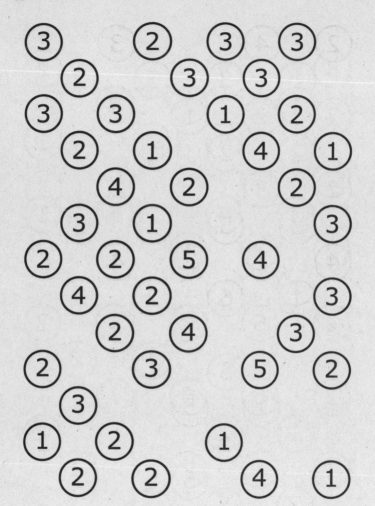

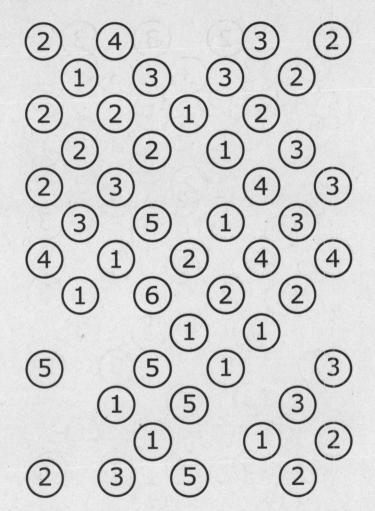

Drastic Puzzles

19

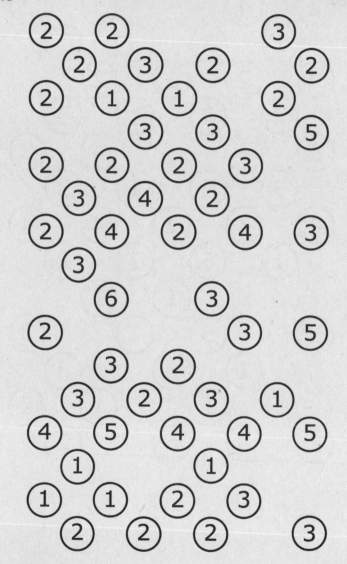

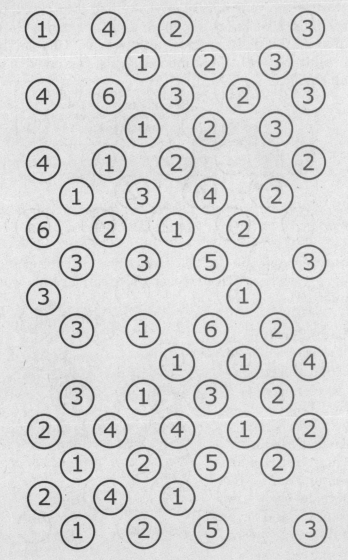

The Su Doku invasion

2005 was the year that Su Dokus invaded. At the start of the year hardly anybody had ever heard of them, and books, newspapers and magazines were allowed to deliver facts and stories completely uncluttered by little numbered grids. But one day it all changed.

> SORRY, BUT WE NOW INTERRUPT THIS BOOK TO BRING YOU AN URGENT NEWSFLASH!

"Nearly every printing machine in the world has been reprogrammed to zap us all with Su Doku puzzles."

Sure enough, Su Dokus suddenly started turning up everywhere! Even Shakespearean drama was infected...

Lady Scrabble
"Fie cos, what ails thee this bright morrow?"

Sir D'koo
"Why, 'tis this devilish riddle. Thou must place ye numbers 1-9 but once in every row, column and even unto ye 3x3 blocks."

Lady Scrabble
"Egad."

As you've probably already seen Su Dokus we're not going to spend ages explaining them all here (you'll find everything you need to know in the *Murderous Maths Su Doku* book), but in case you need a bit of help getting started, Truffles will give you a few tips.

Dead Simple Puzzles

1

		3		9				8
	5		4		1		3	6
		7		4	8		5	9
	9		3		7	8	4	
	4	1	6			7		3
				8	3	1	9	
	8	9	1		2			
6	9	7		5				

Start with the centre block which needs 2,5 and 9. First find a space for the 9 that isn't in the same row or column as any other 9's. Then find where the 5 must go, and then put the 2 in the last empty place. Now find a place for a 3 in the middle column - and it can't be in the bottom block because there's already a 3 in there!

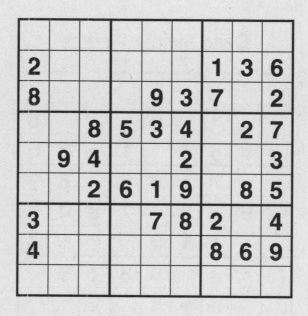

2						1	3	6
8				9	3	7		2
		8	5	3	4		2	7
	9	4			2			3
		2	6	1	9		8	5
3				7	8	2		4
4						8	6	9

You can start by putting all the 3's in!
Remember there should be one (and
only one) 3 in every row, column and
3x3 block. You can also put the
missing 1 and 8 into the right-hand
column and then complete the bottom
right-hand block.

3

	9	1				6	3	
			7		1			
5		6				7		8
	3		5		4		2	
		2				8		
	8		3		6		9	
8		3				5		9
			6		7			
	5	4				2	7	

4

8					3		7	4
	9		5		2	1		8
		3			7		9	
				3		9	4	1
	1				4			
6		7					5	
4		2	3			5		
5				1			2	
	3	1	4					7

5

	4		2		9		5	
	9			5			7	
	8						3	
		2	4	8	1	3		
8		1	5		3	4		7
				4				
9	1						8	5
5		6	7		8	9		3

Devious Puzzles

6

3							7	4
					3			
9		6		8			2	
	2			3	9			6
		9	7	6	5	8		
7			1	4			5	
	4			7		2		9
			6					
6	7							1

You can quickly finish the middle block to start with, and you can also put all the 7's in!

7

	7			4				
			6	2	5			
9		4	3	1				
5							2	
8				3		9	6	4
	4					7	3	
	3					2		
		1	9					8
2				5	3	1		

8

			3				6	
		5		7	2		4	
			1			7	2	
3					5			7
		1	6		8	3		
6			7					5
	5	3			9			
	2		5	1		4		
	4				3			

					5	6		
	8			6			2	
4			9					1
			3					2
6		2	4				1	
8	4	3		2	7	9		
		8	6	1				
7			5				4	
	5		2	7		8		

3		9				4		5
				6				
	2			4			1	
1		5	7		3	2		6
	8						9	
8		4				9		2
	7	1	9		4	8	6	
6			2		8			1

HARDER SU DOKUS

When you move onto harder Su Dokus, you might find that after you've put a few numbers into the grid, you get utterly and completely stuck. You get desperate hoping to find another number to go in, but there are so many possibilities to consider that your mind starts going round in circles and you end up trying out all the same ideas over and over again. In case you need a bit more help, the Murderous Maths Organisation has developed the handy portable "Calcatronic Su Doktor".

If you're too proud to ask a computer for help, our advice is to put the puzzle down and do something else then come back to it. Then with a bit of luck you'll suddenly spot something you hadn't noticed before ... and on you go!

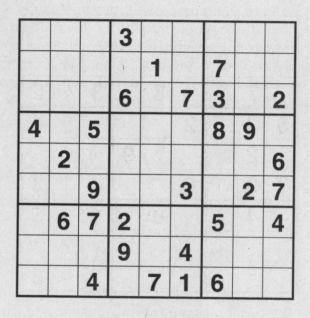

			3					
				1		7		
			6		7	3		2
4		5				8	9	
	2							6
		9			3		2	7
	6	7	2			5		4
			9		4			
		4		7	1	6		

You can complete the bottom middle
block straightaway. Put in the 6, then
the 3 then the 5 and finally the 8.

								7
		2					6	
	7	9		6		3	4	2
5	3		2				8	4
	2				9			
7	9		8				1	3
	4	7		8		1	3	5
		1					2	
								8

6				3	5	9		
5	1		7	6			2	
1			8	5			9	
9	2				1	4	6	
		7			6	3		
			4					
				1		7		
				9	2	6	1	

2			8				3	
	1						5	
			4	6		9		
		3		8				1
7		5	1		2	4		9
9				7		2		
		4		5	3			
	6						2	
	3				8			5

9								
7		1	4					
		6			2	9		
1			2	7		4		
					4			
	3		9		1		6	
2	5					7	1	
	1	7	8					
		4			3		8	5

Drastic Puzzles

4								
			8	2	3			
9	5	8						
		9		8			7	
			5	6	4		9	
3	1			7			5	
2					7	3		
			9			5		
1		5	6			4		9

		8		6	1	7		
7	1	2					9	
		6					4	
8	9		5				6	
	5	3		7				
			6		3	9	7	
9			1	2		8		
	2			8		6		

	7		5		2		3	
8				7				9
	4						5	
			1		6			
		3				1		
4		2	7		3	9		6
		7				5		
	1	6	9		8	2	4	

					1		6	2
				2		9		
			4			1	8	
6	3			8	5			
7		4				5		6
			2	6			3	8
	9	3			2			
		8		9				
4	5		8					

1		2				6		
	5							
			5	7				2
8	1	4						
				4		3		
		3	9			5		
	3		6		2			8
9		7			5		2	
	4				7			3

Eeek! Professor Fiendish isn't too happy that Truffles has being giving tips, so he's just unveiled something rather nasty of his own... It's two Su Dokus glued together, and the numbers in the middle box are the same for both of them. You have to treat it like two separate puzzles, but you'll need to solve them both at the same time.

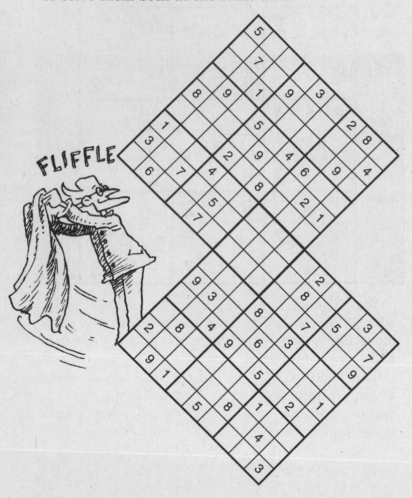

The dreaded Kjarposkos

The Pure Mathematicians at the Murderous Maths Organisation had spent so much time trying to solve Su Dokus and Kakuros that one day they decided to get their revenge. They locked the door to the research lab, then they grabbed a pile of numbers and shapes and performed a series of ghastly experiments on them until suddenly...

Yes! At last they had created something with which they could frustrate the world, and just to make things worse, they gave it the most ridiculous name they could think of.

The KJARPOSKO involves a selection of boxes which are linked together. Each box is divided into two sections, there is a number on top, and you have to fill a number into the answer space underneath.

There's only one rule: *every number on top of a box equals the total of the answers in the bottom of the boxes linked to it.*

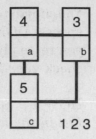

Confused? Don't panic - just look at these three boxes. You need to put the answers 1,2,3 into the spaces indicated by the letters a,b,c. The box with 4 in it is linked to the boxes with the spaces marked b and c. Therefore the numbers you put into b and c must add up to 4. In the same way a+b=5 and a+c=3.

When you fill a number into a space you can cross it off the list at the bottom. Here's the answer:

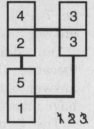

Now we'll try a harder one.

```
[10]---[9]---[12]
 |            |
[14]   [15]  [6]
 |           |
      [8]---[13]
      |
     [  ]
```

1 2 3 4 5 6 7 8

100

You have to fill the numbers 1-8 into the empty spaces. DON'T READ THE NEXT BIT if you think you're ready to solve this puzzle yourself! You can check your answer at the end of the book.

HOW TO SOLVE THIS PUZZLE
Fill in the numbers as you read these instructions

The 14 box is only connected to two others, so the answers in these two must be 6+8. (They can't be 7+7 as all answers are different.) Therefore the 8 box must have an answer of 6 or 8. The 15 box is only connected to two others, so these answers must be 7 + 8. Therefore the 8 box must contain the answer 8.

Immediately the 9 box must have the answer 7 (because 15=8+7) and the 10 box must have the answer 6 (because 14=8+6). Also the 6 box must have answer 5 (because 13=8+5).

The 9 box is connected to the 10 box which already has the answer 6 in it. Therefore the other two boxes it is connected to must have the answers 1 and 2 (9=6+1+2). If answer 1 was in the 12 box, then there must be answer 5 in the 13 box (6=1+5). However we have already used the 5, so this is not possible. Therefore the answer 1 must be in the 15 box and the answer 2 in the 12 box.

Now the rest of the solution is obvious.

TRICKS

The hardest part of Kjarposkos is getting started. If you stare at a puzzle for long enough then eventually you'll realize where one number *has* to go. In the puzzle we just saw, we worked out that the 8 had to go in the "8" box. With harder puzzles this can be quite murderous, so you might prefer to try a few guesses. Before you guess, the secret is to find an empty box that only has a few possibilities. Here are a few tricks to try.

HIGHS AND LOWS

Find the box with the lowest number in it, then check the boxes it is connected to. For instance if a box has "3" on top, you know that the two boxes connected to it can only have 1 or 2 on the bottom. Examining the box with the highest number is also helpful, especially if it is only connected to two others. (We already did this by looking at both the 15 and 14 boxes in the puzzle we've already seen.)

SPLIT THE EVENS

Look for any box that has an even number in it and is only connected to two other boxes. The other two boxes *cannot* contain half of the even number. Eeek! This sounds mad until you look at the diagram below which is a small part of a big puzzle. All we're saying is that 4 is an even number, so you can't put 2 in either the b space or d space. (If you put 2 in space b then you would have to put a 2 in space d because 2+2=4, but you cannot use the same number more than once.) So in this puzzle you would know that either b or d must be 1 and the other must be 3.

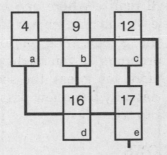

MAX AND MIN (this tip is quite advanced!)

In the diagram above, the 9 box tells us that a+c+d=9. You can make 9 from adding three different numbers in just three ways: 1+3+5 or 2+3+4 or 1+2+6. This tells us that none of a or c or d can be higher than 6.

Now look at the 16 box which tells us a+b+e=16. The maximum possible value of a is 6, and the Split the Evens Tip showed us that the maximum of b is 3. Therefore the *minimum* possible value of e is 7.

If you experiment, you'll find that in this little section of puzzle, the only possible way you can fill in the spaces with no repeating numbers is: a=6 b=3 c=2 d=1 e=7.

If all else fails... GUESS! If you can't see where to start, put in one or two numbers with a pencil and see how they affect the rest of the puzzle. Even if you're wrong this will help find the right answer. Good Luck!

Kjarposko Puzzles

1

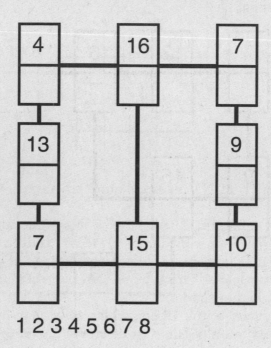

4   16   7

13   9

7   15   10

1 2 3 4 5 6 7 8

The "4" box tells you that the number in the "16" box must be 3 or 1. But if you try 1 you'll find that you can't finish the puzzle using all the numbers 1-8! Therefore the 3 goes in the 16 box. Remember - don't be scared to try numbers out with a pencil, you can always rub them out if they don't work!

TRUFFLES' TIPS

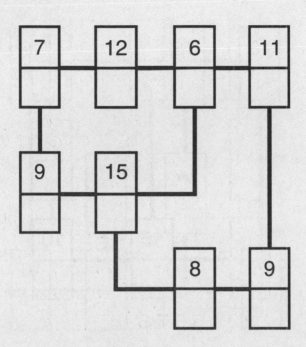

1 2 3 4 5 6 7 8

You can work out what should go in the bottom right "9" box. The "6" box has three connections, so the numbers you put in the boxes that they connect to must be 1+2+3. As the 1, 2, and 3 are now used, the only combination of numbers the "15" box can be connected to are 4+5+6. This means that only numbers 7 and 8 remain to go in the bottom-right box, but if you try 8 then you can't put anything in the "15" box. Therefore what's the only number left...?

TRUFFLES' TIPS

3

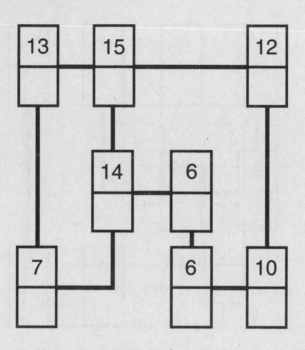

1 2 3 4 5 6 7 8

See the two "6" boxes? These have to be linked to 1+5 and 2+4. Now look at the "13" box. To get 13 you need 6+7 or 5+8, but the 5 has to be linked to a 6 box so it is not available. Therefore you can only make 13 with 6 +7. But the Split the Evens Tip tells you that the 6 cannot go in the "15" box...

4

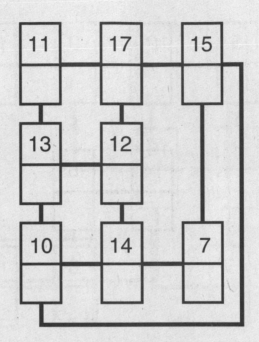

11	17	15
13	12	
10	14	7

1 2 3 4 5 6 7 8

THE FOUR BOX SHORTCUT!
Here's something to look out for when you see four
boxes linked in a ring and one of them isn't
linked to anything else. Look at the
11,17,12 and 13 boxes. The 11 box is only
linked to the 13 and 17 boxes, so we
know the answers in these boxes
must add up to 11. The 12 box is linked
to these same two boxes, but also to
the 14 box. Therefore the number in
the 14 box must be 12-11 = 1.

5

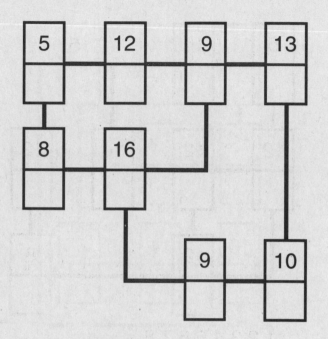

5	12	9	13
8	16		
		9	10

1 2 3 4 5 6 7 8

What goes in the 5 box? It's in-between 12 and 8, so it cannot be 4 or 6 because of the Split the Evens Tip. The 8 box means it cannot be 8, and if you try 1,2 or 3 then you can't put anything in the 9 box. Therefore the 5 box can only contain 5 or 7. Now try 7 with a pencil and see what happens...

TRUFFLES' TIPS

6

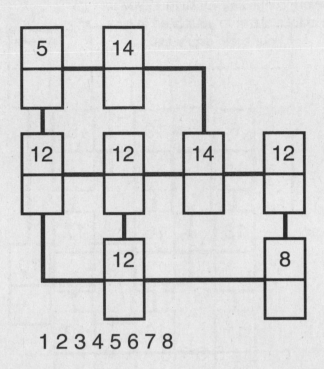

12345678

What is the only number that can go in the 14 box on the middle row? You might be able to do this in your head. Try all the numbers 1-8 and see how this affects the number in the 5 box. If you find a number that works, before you write it in, check what goes into the 8 box!

TRUFFLES' TIPS

WARNING!
Now you've had some practise,
things are going to get much tougher.
Before continuing we suggest you fix
a smoke alarm to your head in case
your brain overheats.

7

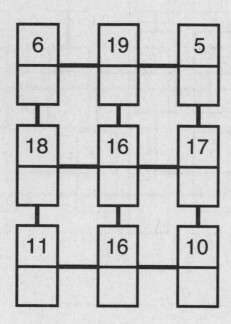

1 2 3 4 5 6 7 8 9

The easiest place to start here is to
see what might go into the 19 box,
then fill in the 18, 17 and bottom 16
boxes. Then try and fill in the three
boxes connected to the 16 box at the
bottom with the unused numbers.

8

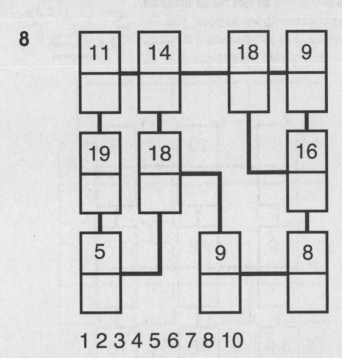

1 2 3 4 5 6 7 8 10

Here's something to watch out for. The 11 box must contain 9 or 10 (because of the 19 box). If you put 9 in the 11 box, then the numbers in the two 18 boxes must add to 5 (because of the 14 box). However the numbers in the central 18 box and the 19 box must also add to 5 (because of the 5 box). This is called a CLASH! Suppose you put 1 in the central 18 box, then both the other 18 box and the 19 box will need a 4 which you can't do. In fact you can't put anything in the 18 box and then fill in the other two boxes. Therefore ... the 11 box must contain the 10!

TRUFFLES' TIPS

9

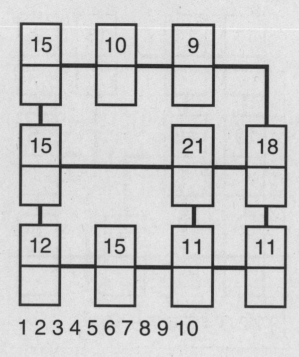

15 10 9

15   21 18

12 15 11 11

1 2 3 4 5 6 7 8 9 10

You can use the Four Box Shortcut here!

TRUFFLES' TIPS

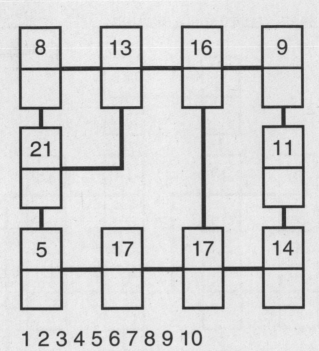

| 8 | 13 | 16 | 9 |

| 21 | | | 11 |

| 5 | 17 | 17 | 14 |

1 2 3 4 5 6 7 8 9 10

Just for practise - imagine putting 8 into the 17 box on the right. The 16 box then tells you that the numbers in the 13 box and 9 box must add to 8. However the 8 box tells you that the numbers in the 13 box and 21 box also add to 8. It's a CLASH! Therefore you cannot put 8 into the right-hand 17 box.

TRUFFLES' TIPS

WARNING!
These puzzles are now becoming as difficult as drastic Kakuros!

BRAIN TEMPERATURE: SIZZLING

PEEP PEEP PEEP

11

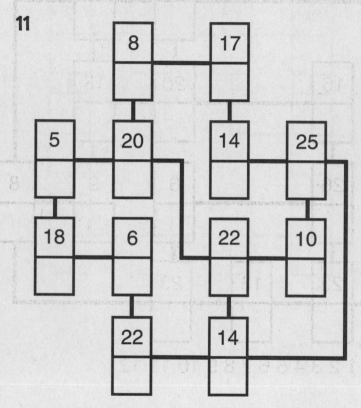

1 2 3 4 5 6 7 8 9 10 11 12

TRUFFLES' TIPS

You can use the Four Box Shortcut here! If you can find it, you'll see what number has to go in the 22 box.

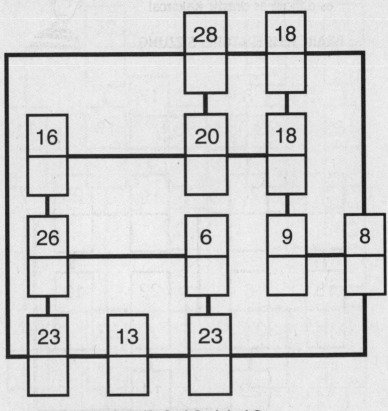

28 18

16 20 18

26 6 9 8

23 13 23

1 2 3 4 5 6 7 8 9 10 11 12

Once again, the Four Box Shortcut might save your brain here, and don't forget to look out for more Four Box Shortcuts in the later puzzles. Sorry, this is the last tip I can give you! From now on you're ON YOUR OWN!

13

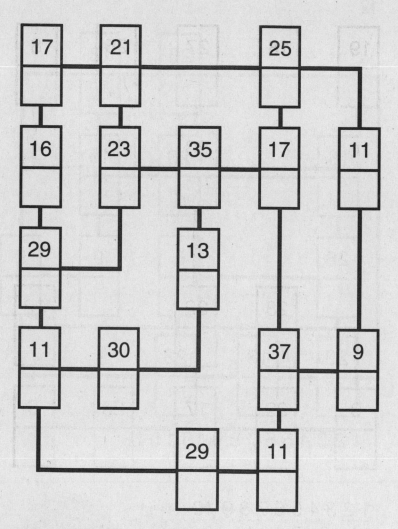

1 2 3 4 5 6 7 8 9 10
11 12 13 14 15 16

14

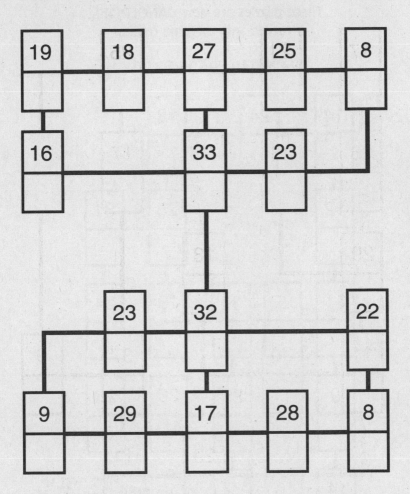

1 2 3 4 5 6 7 8 9 10
11 12 13 14 15 16

WARNING!
These puzzles are now DANGEROUS!
Proceed with extreme caution.

BRAIN TEMPERATURE: CRITICAL

15

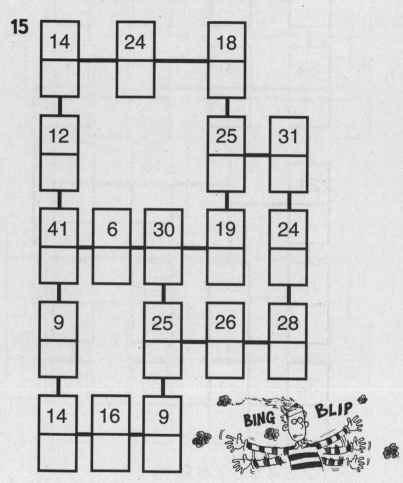

1 2 3 4 5 6 7 8 9 10 11
12 13 14 15 16 17 18

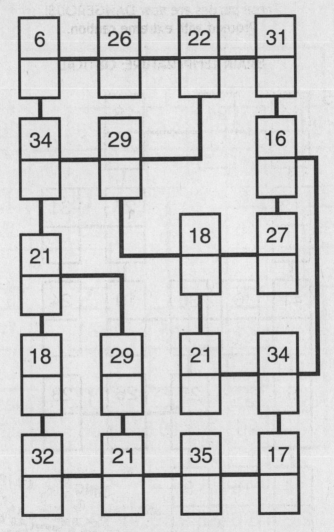

1 2 3 4 5 6 7 8 9 10 11
12 13 14 15 16 17 18

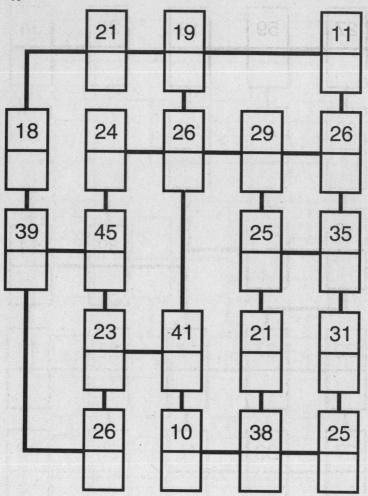

1 2 3 4 5 6 7 8 9 10 11 12
13 14 15 16 17 18 19 20

18

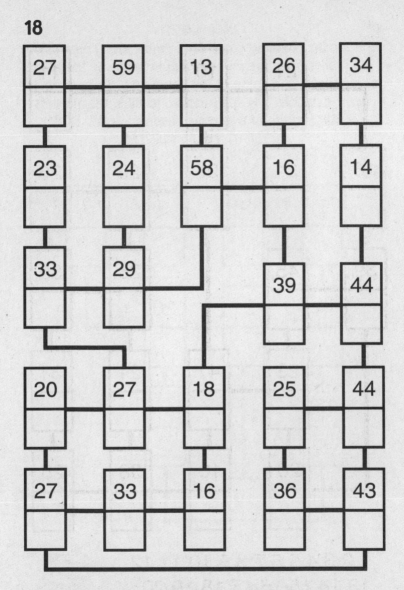

1 2 3 4 5 6 7 8 9 10 11 12 13 14
15 16 17 18 19 20 21 22 23 24

WARNING!

You are approaching some of the most lethal puzzles on the planet. They are so hard that they are on the edge of meltdown and some of the numbers have evaporated into * symbols. It is still possible to fill in the answers but if you are of a nervous disposition DO NOT ATTEMPT THESE PUZZLES.

19

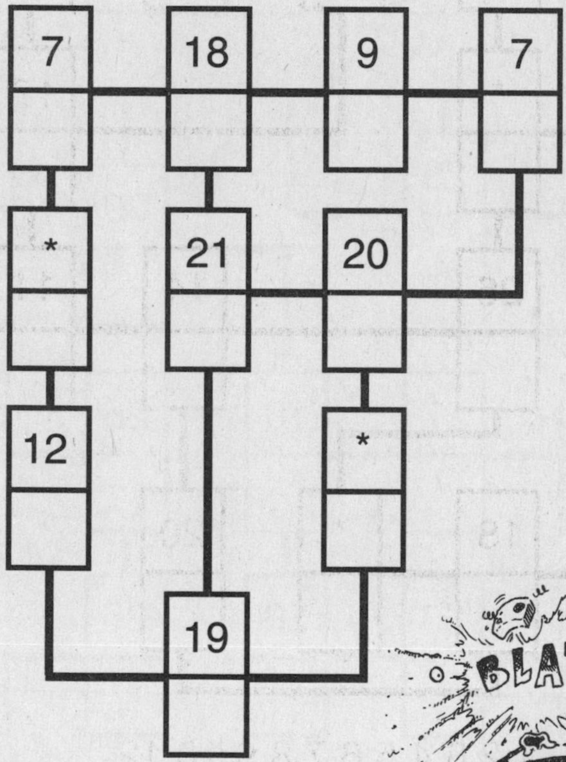
7
18
9
7
*
21
20
12
*
19

BLATT

1 2 3 4 5 6 7 8 9 10

20

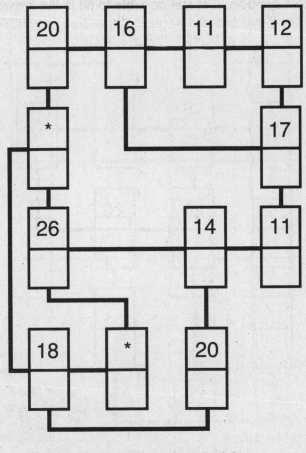

1 2 3 4 5 6 7 8 9 10 12

123

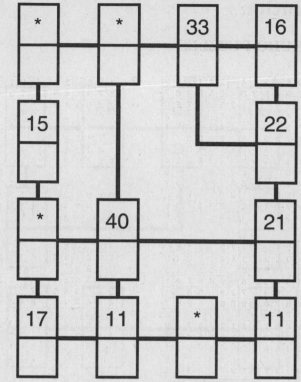

*	*	33	16
15			22
*	40		21
17	11	*	11

1 2 3 4 5 6 7 8 9 10 11 12 13

There! That's the last of the Kjarposkos. If you managed to complete them all then CONGRATULATIONS! You have won a Star Prize from Pongo McWhiffy's Deluxe Burger bar... but you'll never guess what mystery flavour it is!

Solutions

KAKURO PUZZLES

1

9	8		2	1	4		2	4	1		5	9
7	9	8	6	3	5		6	5	3	9	8	7
	7	9		1	2	3			7	9		
2	1			2	4	1			6	2		
1	3		2	6		4	3		3	1		
4	2	5	9	1	3		5	1	2	3	7	4
	9	8						1	5			
2	4	6	7	9	8		6	7	8	9	5	4
1	6		7	9		5	9		6	2		
4	8		6	4	1		3	1				
	9	8		1	2	3		9	8			
8	7	9	1	3	2		2	1	3	7	9	8
9	5		2	1	4		4	2	1		7	9

2

1	5	8		2	1			2	1		
3	7	9		4	3	5		1	3	4		
	3	6	2	1		2	1	3		1	2	4
7	9		1	3		1	3		7	8	9	
9	8	5	6		1	3		6	8	2	9	7
	1	3	2	4		7	9		4	6		
6	4	2		1	3		7	9		6	1	8
9	2		1	3		6	8	9	7			
1	3	8	2	4		2	9		8	9	6	7
2	1	3		2	1		2	1		8	9	
8	6	9		2	1	3		1	3	2	5	
	4	2	1		5	2	4		1	7	3	
	1	3			1	3		3	9	8		

3

2	1			1	3	2			1	5		
1	3	5	2		2	1	4		7	3	4	2
2	1		6	9	8		7	9	8		1	3
4	5	8	9	7	6		9	8	6	7	2	1
		9	5		7	9	8		9	8		
9	6	7	8		9	8	6		5	9	8	7
7	9								9	8		
6	8	9	7		4	1	2		8	7	5	9
	8	9		2	3	1		9	8			
2	1	6	8	7	9		6	8	5	9	2	1
1	3		6	9	8		8	9	7		1	3
4	2	1	5		5	9	7		6	3	4	2
	4	3			7	6	9			1	5	

4

9	8			8	4		2	1			2	1
7	9	8		6	2	1	5	3		2	1	3
	7	9	8		3	2	1		5	1	3	
		3	5	6	1		6	1	2	3		
2	6		9	8	6		7	3	1		5	1
4	8	6	7	9	5		8	5	4	9	7	3
	9	8							8	9		
3	7	9	5	8	4		7	9	4	6	8	3
1	5		3	7	1		1	5	2		6	1
		3	1	6	2		3	8	1	2		
	3	1	2		3	1	2		3	1	2	
3	1	2		1	5	2	4	3		3	1	2
1	2			3	6		5	1			3	1

5

	9	8		2	1	8	6	9		2	1	3
4	6	1		1	3	9	8	7		4	2	1
9	8	2	7	3		7	9		9	1		
		6	9	8		5	7	9	8		7	9
3	1		6	9	8		3	5	7	9	8	
1	2	8	5		7	9		7	9	8	6	
	3	5		9	8	5		8	6			
8	9	7	5		7	9		2	5	3	1	
6	8	9	1	3		2	3	1		4	2	
9	7		2	1	8	6		9	8	6		
		1	3		1	3		7	4	3	8	9
2	1	4		3	7	9	1	8		9	6	8
1	3	2		1	9	8	2	6		7	9	

6

3	1		9	7		9	7		3	1
9	7	8	5	6		5	6	8	9	7
8	9	6		9	5	8		6	8	9
1	2		8	9	7		1	2		
7	3	4	2			6	5	7	3	
	1	3	2		1	4	2			
	2	1	4		3	2	1			
6	8	3	5			1	3	6	8	
2	1		7	6	9		2	1		
9	7	8	9	8	6		8	9	7	
8	9	6	7	5		5	7	6	8	9
1	3		9	8		8	9		1	3

7

```
9 8 4 6 7 . 4 1 3 2 6
7 9 6 8 5 . 5 2 1 6 8
3 1 . . 8 9 6 . . 7 9
2 4 1 . 9 7 8 . 2 1 4
1 6 3 4 . . 2 1 3 7 .
. . . 9 8 . 9 8 . . .
. . . 7 9 . 7 9 . . .
6 1 3 2 . . . 7 8 6 9
4 2 1 . 8 9 6 . 9 3 7
1 3 . . 9 7 8 . . 1 3
9 7 8 5 6 . 3 8 1 2 4
8 9 6 7 4 . 7 9 3 4 8
```

8

```
4 2 . 9 7 . 9 7 . 4 2
9 7 8 5 6 . 5 6 8 9 7
8 9 6 . 8 9 6 . 6 8 9
2 1 . . 2 4 1 . . 2 1
1 3 . 6 9 7 8 4 . 1 3
. 1 3 . . . 1 3 . .
. 2 1 . . . 2 1 . .
6 8 . 2 3 9 7 5 . 6 8
1 3 . . 1 6 3 . . 1 3
9 7 8 . 6 8 9 . 8 9 7
8 9 6 7 5 . 5 7 6 8 9
2 1 . 9 8 . 8 9 . 2 1
```

9

```
8 4 3 9 . 8 9 . . 8 9
4 2 1 7 . 9 7 8 . 9 7
3 1 . 8 7 . . 9 7 6 8
9 6 8 . 9 5 8 . 9 5 .
7 3 5 9 . 9 7 2 . 1 3
. . 7 8 9 . 3 1 5 2 4
9 8 1 2 6 . 9 6 8 . .
7 9 . 1 3 2 . 4 9 3 7
. 4 3 . 5 1 2 . 3 1 2
4 2 1 3 . . 1 2 . 7 9
1 3 . 6 8 9 . 1 7 2 6
2 1 . . 9 7 . 3 9 6 8
```

10

```
. 9 4 5 . . 9 8 . 7 9 .
9 8 1 3 . 4 6 5 9 8 7
5 7 2 1 4 . 7 9 . 5 9
. . 7 9 8 6 5 . 9 7 .
3 1 5 . 7 9 . 1 3 . .
1 2 . . 9 8 . 2 4 3 1
2 4 3 1 . 7 4 . . 1 2
. 1 2 . 3 1 . 1 2 4
. 8 2 . 4 5 2 1 3 .
9 5 . 9 7 . 6 9 8 4 3
8 7 9 5 6 4 . 7 9 2 1
. 9 8 . 8 9 . 5 6 1 .
```

11

```
9 8 . 7 9 . . 9 8 .
7 9 . 6 8 9 . 7 6 8
8 6 7 9 . 8 7 . 7 9
. . 6 8 9 . 8 7 9 6
. 7 9 . 7 8 5 9 . .
7 9 8 6 . 7 9 . 7 9
9 8 . 5 9 . 6 7 9 8
. . 9 8 7 6 . 9 8 .
8 6 7 9 . 7 9 8 . .
9 7 . 7 8 . 7 6 9 8
6 9 7 . 9 7 6 . 8 6
. 8 9 . . 9 8 . 7 9
```

12

```
. 3 1 . . . 3 4 .
5 1 2 3 . . 3 1 2 5
7 9 . 2 6 8 1 . 1 7
9 8 7 . 8 9 . 8 7 9
8 6 9 . 9 7 . 6 9 8
. . 6 7 . . 8 9 . .
. . 8 9 . . 9 7 . .
1 2 3 . 9 7 . 1 4 2
2 4 1 . 8 9 . 3 2 1
3 1 . 5 6 8 9 . 1 3
5 9 8 7 . . 7 8 9 5
. 7 9 . . . 9 7 .
```

13

```
. 3 1 . . . 3 4 .
5 1 2 3 . . 3 1 2 7
7 9 . 2 6 8 1 . 1 5
9 8 7 . 8 9 . 8 7 9
8 6 9 . 9 7 . 6 9 8
. . 6 7 . . 9 7 . .
. . 8 9 . . 8 9 . .
1 2 3 . 7 9 . 1 4 2
2 4 1 . 9 8 . 3 2 1
3 1 . 7 8 6 9 . 1 3
5 6 8 9 . . 7 8 9 4
. 7 9 . . . 9 7 .
```

14

```
. 5 1 . 2 1 . 7 5 .
2 4 3 . 1 3 . 8 9 6
1 3 . 1 4 2 8 . 7 9
4 1 3 2 . . 9 7 6 8
. 2 1 . . . 9 8 .
. . 4 3 . . 9 5 .
. 2 1 . . 7 6 . .
5 9 . . . . 1 8 .
2 4 7 1 . . 7 8 9 6
1 3 . 7 8 6 9 . 7 9
4 1 3 . 7 9 . 7 6 8
. 2 1 . 9 8 . 9 5 .
```

15
```
9 6 8 . . . . 1 2 3
1 2 9 3 . . . 8 3 6 9
3 1 . 8 7 9 6 . 1 5
. 3 8 . 9 8 . 1 3
. . 7 9 . . 7 9
. . 9 8 . . 9 8
. 8 6 . 7 9 . 3 2
1 3 . 7 9 8 6 . 7 9
2 6 1 3 . . 7 9 4 8
3 9 5 . . . 5 1 7
```

16
```
1 3 . . 1 3 . 3 2 1
6 8 . 1 2 4 . 1 4 2
9 7 8 6 . 2 1 . 5 3
8 9 6 . 4 1 3 2 6 .
2 1 . 3 1 . 5 1 .
. 1 5 . 1 2 . 7 3
. 7 3 2 1 4 . 8 9 7
1 3 . 1 3 . 7 6 8 9
2 8 1 . 4 3 9 . 3 1
4 9 6 . 2 1 . . 1 2
```

17
```
6 9 8 . . . . 9 6 8
2 1 9 3 . . 3 7 1 2
1 3 . 5 1 2 4 . 4 9
. 2 4 . 3 1 . 3 2
. . 1 2 . . 1 2
. . 3 1 . . 3 1
. 7 9 . 1 2 . 4 2
1 3 . 6 3 1 9 . 7 9
4 9 6 8 . . 7 9 3 8
2 8 1 . . . 4 1 6
```

18
```
. . 2 1 . . 7 9 .
4 2 1 3 . . 9 8 3 7
1 3 . 5 7 9 8 . 1 3
2 1 5 . 9 8 . 8 6 9
. 8 9 7 . . 8 7 9
. 6 8 9 . . 6 9 8
8 5 7 . 7 9 . 5 2 1
9 7 . 7 9 8 2 . 5 3
6 9 7 8 . . 3 1 4 2
. 9 5 . . 1 2 .
```

19
```
. 5 9 . 4 3 . 6 9 8
9 8 7 . 5 1 6 8 7 9
7 9 . 1 3 . 7 9 .
. 6 4 2 1 3 . 7 2 4
. 9 4 2 1 3 . 3 1
2 4 1 . . 2 1 . 1 2
3 1 . 9 8 . . 2 5 3
1 2 . 5 7 1 2 3 .
5 3 9 . 9 2 4 1 8
. 5 9 . 3 1 . 9 8
8 9 6 7 1 5 . 8 7 9
9 7 8 . 3 4 . 9 5
```

20
```
9 8 7 5 . . 1 3 8 9
8 6 9 7 . . 2 1 9 7
7 9 . 4 1 2 3 . 6 8
5 7 8 . 3 1 . 9 7 5
. . 1 2 . 1 2 .
. . 3 1 . 3 1 .
7 5 9 . 1 2 . 4 3 5
6 8 . 4 3 1 2 . 1 3
9 7 8 5 . . 3 1 4 2
8 9 6 7 . . 5 3 2 1
```

21
```
. . 7 9 . . 9 8 .
7 6 9 8 . . 7 9 6 8
9 8 . 5 9 7 8 . 7 9
. 2 5 4 8 9 6 3 1
8 7 9 . . . 1 2 3
6 9 8 . . . 2 4 1
. 1 7 2 5 8 6 4 9
1 3 . 5 7 9 8 . 3 1
2 4 1 3 . . 9 8 5 2
. . 2 1 . . 7 9 .
```

22
```
2 3 6 1 . 1 2 . 2 1
4 5 9 2 . 3 6 8 7 9
. 7 8 4 9 6 . 6 9 8
7 9 . . 7 2 9 . 1 3
9 8 7 6 5 . 7 9 .
. 9 8 . 5 6 8 9 7
2 5 . 9 2 7 . 8 9
8 9 7 . 6 9 8 4 7
6 8 9 7 3 . 6 1 3 2
9 7 . 2 1 . 9 2 5 4
```

23

8	9	7		9	8		9	8	6
6	8	9		7	9		7	9	8
9	7		9	8	6	7		7	9
1	6	2	3			6	9	5	7
		5	1			8	5		
		1	2			3	7		
5	7	9	8			9	8	7	5
8	6		6	4	2	5		9	7
9	8	6		2	1		9	6	8
7	9	8		1	3		7	8	9

24

	5	3	1	2		1	3	8	9
3	7	1	2	4		2	1	9	7
8	9		3	1	2	4		2	1
		6	4		1	3		7	2
	4	8		2	4		7	6	
	7	9		1	3		9	5	
3	5		1	3		4	8		
1	3		2	4	1	3		1	3
2	1	3	4		2	1	3	5	4
4	2	5	9		4	2	1	3	

25

1	2	4		4	7	9		1	3
3	1	5	9	6	8	7		2	1
		9	8	7			8	5	
7	5	8		1	2		9	7	5
8	9		2	9	7	1		8	9
9	7		1	8	9	3		9	7
6	8	9		3	1		3	6	8
	6	7			3	2	1		
1	2		9	7	4	1	5	2	3
3	1		8	9	6		2	4	1

26

1	3		6	9	8		9	8	7		1	3
2	1	6	8	7	9		5	9	6	8	2	1
		8	9		5	8	6		8	9		
		9	7		7	9	8		9	7		
3	1			8	4		4	8			3	1
4	5	1	3	6	2		2	6	3	1	4	5
		2	1	4				4	1	2		
1	3	4	2	9	8		8	9	2	4	1	3
2	1			7	9		9	7			2	1
		9	8		4	3	1		9	8		
		7	9		2	1	4		7	9		
1	2	8	6	9	7		7	9	8	6	1	2
3	1		3	7	5		5	8	6		3	1

27

9	7		5	9		8	9			4	5	9
6	3	9	8	7		9	7		9	1	3	7
2	1	7	9		9	7		9	7	2	1	4
		3	1	2	4		8	5		4	8	
8	6	5		1	3	2		6	8	5		
9	7		9	3		8	9			9	8	
6	9	7	8		8	9	7		8	7	9	6
	8	9			9	7		9	7		7	9
		8	5	1		6	9	7		9	6	8
6	2		2	3			8	6	9	7		
7	3	9	1	2		8	7		1	3	8	9
9	6	8	3		8	9		3	2	1	4	7
5	1	6		9	7		1	5		1	3	

28

3	7	9	1	8		3	1	9	8	7
1	9	8	2	6		1	2	8	6	9
	1	6		7	9	8		7	9	
1	2	7		9	8	6		5	3	1
3	4		2	5		2	3		7	2
		1	3				1	3		
		2	1				2	1		
3	4		9	5		3	4		3	1
1	2	6		7	9	8		5	4	2
	1	3		9	8	6		7	9	
3	7	9	1	8		2	1	8	6	9
1	9	8	2	6		1	3	9	8	7

29

	9	6	8		7	9		5	8
9	8	3	1		6	8	5	9	7
7	6	1	2	3	4		6	8	9
		2	4	1		3	1	6	2
	6	5	7		4	1	2		
7	9		6	7	9			7	9
9	8			9	8	7		9	8
		8	9	6		6	8	5	
4	8	9	7		2	3	5		
2	1	4		7	6	8	9	4	3
1	3	5	2	4		9	7	2	1
5	2		1	3		2	4	1	

30

	5	7		9	7		5	8	7	9
5	8	9	7	6	2		7	6	9	8
9	7		9	8		8	9		1	2
	9	7		5	9	7			3	1
1	4	9	7		8	9	7		8	6
3	6	8	9	7		1	2	6		
		2	4	1		6	4	9	7	1
6	8		8	3	1		6	8	9	3
2	1			2	5	4		1	3	
1	3		1	4		1	2		8	9
8	9	6	7		2	3	1	4	6	7
9	7	1	2		1	5		2	1	

31

5	7		8	3			4	2	1	3
8	6		9	7	8		2	1	3	5
7	9	8	4	1	6		1	3		
9	8	6			5	4	7	9	8	6
	4	8	6	9	7		7	9	8	
5	7		6	9		8	9		7	9
7	9		9	7		9	7		5	7
9	8	7		8	9	6	5	3		
8	6	9	4	5	7			9	8	6
	1	3		6	1	4	7	9	8	
5	3	2	1		8	7	9		7	9
9	1	4	2			3	8		5	7

32

3	1	2	9	7		3	2	1	9	7
1	2	4	8	9		1	4	2	8	9
9	7			6	8	9			3	1
8	9			8	9	7			1	2
	1	2	4		4	1	2			
2	1	9	7			8	9	6	7	
1	3	8	9			9	7	8	5	
	3	1	4		2	3	1			
8	9			6	8	9			1	2
9	7			8	9	7			3	1
3	1	2	9	7		3	2	1	9	7
1	2	4	8	9		1	4	2	8	9

33

	4	9		3	4		3	1		3	1	
9	6	8		1	2		1	2		9	4	6
7	1	4	2		5	4	9		4	6	2	1
	6	1		3	1	2		9	8			
	2	1		1	2	4		2	9			
4	1	3	5	2	6		5	8	6	1	4	2
1	3		3	1			7	9		3	1	
2	4	7	9	8	6		5	9	8	6	1	4
	5	9		5	4	9		4	2			
	3	9		3	1	2		1	2			
3	9	5	8		1	2	4		3	1	2	9
1	3	2		3	4		3	1		9	6	8
	5	1		1	2		1	2		3	1	

34

	1	2		8	4		1	4	2
6	4	9		6	3		3	2	1
1	2	8	5	9	7			1	3
	7	9		2	1	9	3	5	
8	9	6		6	9	8			
3	7	1	8		1	3		8	7
9	6		6	1		7	8	9	5
	1	4	2			4	2	1	
5	7	3	9	6		1	3		
8	6		4	3	5	2	1	9	
9	8	6		7	2		6	9	8
7	9	8		5	1		1	3	

35

	8	6	9	3		6	3	9	8
	6	2	7	1		3	1	7	9
	9	7		4	1	2		3	1
2	4	1		2	3	1		2	4	1
1	7	3	2			4	1	6	3
			4	8	1	3	2		
			5	9	2	1	6		
7	9	4	8			5	6	1	3
9	8	6		2	4	1		4	2	1
	7	9		1	2	3		1	3
	3	1	9	7		6	1	9	7
	1	2	7	4		2	3	8	9

36

1	2	3	5		2	1			
2	4	1	3		5	3	1	2	4
3	1		7	9		5	3	1	2
9	7		4	7	9	2		3	1
	2	1	3	7		7	9		
9	8	4	2	1		1	5	3	
3	5	1		1	2	4	8	9	
	9	7		7	3	1	2		
1	3		8	9	7	4		3	5
2	1	3	7		9	7		1	3
4	2	1	5	3		3	1	4	2
			9	7		5	3	2	1

37

4	9	7		9	8		7	9		7	9	4
2	5	1	3	7	4		6	5	7	9	8	2
1	8	9	6		9	6	8		6	5	3	1
	3	2		5	7	8	9	6		8	6	
9	7		4	1	2		1	2	4		7	9
8	6	9	7	3	1		3	1	6	4	5	8
		8	9					8	7			
8	5	6	3	7	1		3	1	7	9	4	2
9	7		8	9	7		8	2	9		3	1
	3	5		5	2	3	1	4		2	8	
7	2	1	4		4	1	2		3	1	2	8
9	4	6	8	7	5		6	8	4	5	7	9
8	1	3		9	8		7	9		3	1	6

38

	7	9		9	5		5	1		5	7	
9	3	5		7	6		4	3		7	9	1
8	1	2	3		8	9	6		7	9	8	3
	2	4	1		1	4	2		9	8	6	
3	4		5	9	7	1	2			3	1	
1	5	6	2	3	7		3	8	9	6	5	2
		8	9	6				4	2	1		
8	5	2	4	1	3		2	1	4	3	6	7
9	7		2	5	6	1	3			5	9	
	6	8	9		9	8	6		9	6	8	
2	8	9	7		7	9	8		7	8	9	3
1	9	7		7	6		7	9		9	7	1
	1	2		9	8		9	8		1	2	

39

8	6	9			1	2	4
2	1	6	4		8	2	9	7
1	3	8	9		6	4	8	9
9	2		8	7	9	5		4	6
6	4	8		9	8		2	1	8
		7	9		7	9	
	9	8		9	8	
1	8	2		7	9		7	6	4
4	6		3	9	8	2		8	1
9	7	2	1		1	2	7	9
8	9	4	6		6	4	9	8
2	4	1			1	4	2

40

	8	6	9	7	4		7	5
	3	1	4	8	9	2		9	7
3	1	2		5	2	1	9	6	8
2	6		4	7	3		7	8	9
	4	1	2		6	7	
1	2	3	5		8	9		7	9
3	5		3	4		6	7	9	8
	1	2		8	9	6
1	2	3		7	3	5		1	2
2	4	1	9	8	5		1	3	4
3	1		6	3	1	4	2	5
8	9		8	1	2	6	9

BRIDGE PUZZLES

Here is how the starting puzzle on page 54 should look when you've finished:

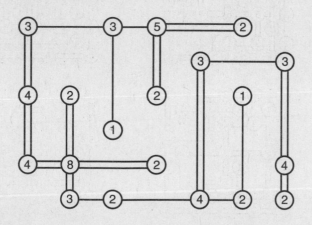

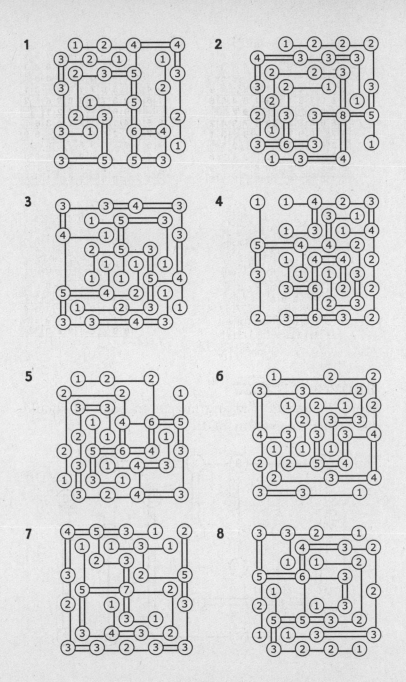

131

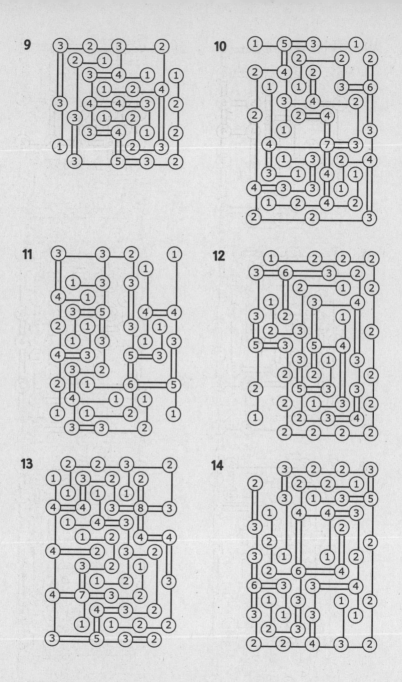

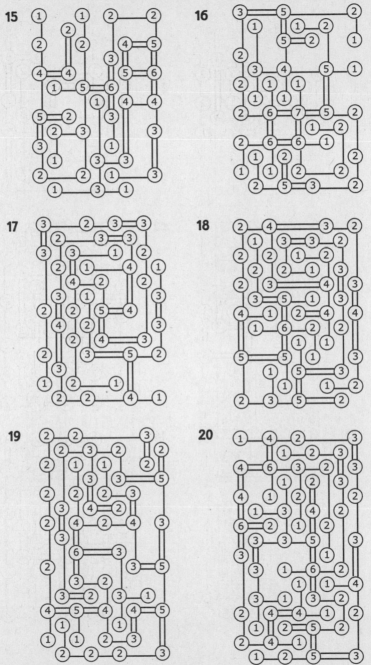

133

SU DOKU PUZZLES

1

9	4	1	8	3	6	5	7	2
6	7	3	5	9	2	4	1	8
8	5	2	4	7	1	9	3	6
3	1	7	2	4	8	6	5	9
2	9	6	3	5	7	8	4	1
5	8	4	1	6	9	7	2	3
4	2	5	6	8	3	1	9	7
7	3	8	9	1	4	2	6	5
1	6	9	7	2	5	3	8	4

2

1	4	3	2	6	7	5	9	8
2	7	9	8	4	5	1	3	6
8	5	6	1	9	3	7	4	2
6	1	8	5	3	4	9	2	7
5	9	4	7	8	2	6	1	3
7	3	2	6	1	9	4	8	5
3	6	1	9	7	8	2	5	4
4	2	7	3	5	1	8	6	9
9	8	5	4	2	6	3	7	1

3

7	9	1	8	4	5	6	3	2
3	2	8	7	6	1	9	4	5
5	4	6	2	9	3	7	1	8
9	3	7	5	8	4	1	2	6
4	6	2	1	7	9	8	5	3
1	8	5	3	2	6	4	9	7
8	7	3	4	1	2	5	6	9
2	1	9	6	5	7	3	8	4
6	5	4	9	3	8	2	7	1

4

8	5	6	1	9	3	2	7	4
7	9	4	5	6	2	1	3	8
1	2	3	8	4	7	6	9	5
2	8	5	7	3	6	9	4	1
3	1	9	2	5	4	7	8	6
6	4	7	9	8	1	3	5	2
4	6	2	3	7	8	5	1	9
5	7	8	6	1	9	4	2	3
9	3	1	4	2	5	8	6	7

5

6	4	7	2	3	9	8	5	1
1	9	3	8	5	6	2	7	4
2	8	5	1	7	4	6	3	9
7	5	2	4	8	1	3	9	6
4	3	9	6	2	7	5	1	8
8	6	1	5	9	3	4	2	7
3	7	8	9	4	5	1	6	2
9	1	4	3	6	2	7	8	5
5	2	6	7	1	8	9	4	3

6

3	8	2	5	9	6	1	7	4
4	5	7	2	1	3	6	9	8
9	1	6	4	8	7	3	2	5
5	2	4	8	3	9	7	1	6
1	3	9	7	6	5	8	4	2
7	6	8	1	4	2	9	5	3
8	4	5	3	7	1	2	6	9
2	9	1	6	5	8	4	3	7
6	7	3	9	2	4	5	8	1

7

6	7	2	8	4	9	5	1	3
3	1	8	6	2	5	4	9	7
9	5	4	3	1	7	6	8	2
5	9	3	7	6	4	8	2	1
8	2	7	5	3	1	9	6	4
1	4	6	2	9	8	7	3	5
7	3	5	1	8	6	2	4	9
4	6	1	9	7	2	3	5	8
2	8	9	4	5	3	1	7	6

8

2	1	7	3	9	4	5	6	8
9	6	5	8	7	2	1	4	3
4	3	8	1	5	6	7	2	9
3	8	2	9	4	5	6	1	7
5	7	1	6	2	8	3	9	4
6	9	4	7	3	1	2	8	5
1	5	3	4	6	9	8	7	2
8	2	9	5	1	7	4	3	6
7	4	6	2	8	3	9	5	1

9

2	1	7	8	4	5	6	3	9
3	8	9	7	6	1	5	2	4
4	6	5	9	3	2	7	8	1
5	9	1	3	8	6	4	7	2
6	7	2	4	5	9	3	1	8
8	4	3	1	2	7	9	6	5
9	3	8	6	1	4	2	5	7
7	2	6	5	9	8	1	4	3
1	5	4	2	7	3	8	9	6

10

3	6	9	8	1	7	4	2	5
4	1	8	5	6	2	7	3	9
5	2	7	3	4	9	6	1	8
1	4	5	7	9	3	2	8	6
7	8	6	1	2	5	3	9	4
9	3	2	4	8	6	1	5	7
8	5	4	6	3	1	9	7	2
2	7	1	9	5	4	8	6	3
6	9	3	2	7	8	5	4	1

11

7	4	2	3	8	5	9	6	1
3	9	6	4	1	2	7	8	5
1	5	8	6	9	7	3	4	2
4	7	5	1	2	6	8	9	3
8	2	3	7	4	9	1	5	6
6	1	9	8	5	3	4	2	7
9	6	7	2	3	8	5	1	4
5	3	1	9	6	4	2	7	8
2	8	4	5	7	1	6	3	9

12

6	1	3	4	2	8	5	9	7
4	5	2	7	9	3	8	6	1
8	7	9	1	6	5	3	4	2
5	3	6	2	1	7	9	8	4
1	2	8	3	4	9	7	5	6
7	9	4	8	5	6	2	1	3
9	4	7	6	8	2	1	3	5
3	8	1	5	7	4	6	2	9
2	6	5	9	3	1	4	7	8

13

3	7	9	2	4	8	1	5	6
6	8	2	1	3	5	9	7	4
5	1	4	7	6	9	8	2	3
1	3	6	8	5	4	2	9	7
9	2	8	3	7	1	4	6	5
4	5	7	9	2	6	3	8	1
2	6	1	4	8	7	5	3	9
8	9	5	6	1	3	7	4	2
7	4	3	5	9	2	6	1	8

14

2	9	7	8	1	5	6	3	4
4	1	6	3	2	9	8	5	7
3	5	8	4	6	7	9	1	2
6	2	3	9	8	4	5	7	1
7	8	5	1	3	2	4	6	9
9	4	1	5	7	6	2	8	3
8	7	4	2	5	3	1	9	6
5	6	9	7	4	1	3	2	8
1	3	2	6	9	8	7	4	5

15

9	2	3	5	8	7	1	4	6
7	8	1	4	9	6	3	5	2
5	4	6	1	3	2	9	7	8
1	6	5	2	7	8	4	3	9
8	7	9	3	6	4	5	2	1
4	3	2	9	5	1	8	6	7
2	5	8	6	4	9	7	1	3
3	1	7	8	2	5	6	9	4
6	9	4	7	1	3	2	8	5

16

4	3	2	7	9	5	6	8	1
7	6	1	8	2	3	9	4	5
9	5	8	4	1	6	7	3	2
5	4	9	3	8	1	2	7	6
8	2	7	5	6	4	1	9	3
3	1	6	2	7	9	8	5	4
2	9	4	1	5	7	3	6	8
6	8	3	9	4	2	5	1	7
1	7	5	6	3	8	4	2	9

17

6	3	9	2	4	7	1	5	8
5	4	8	9	6	1	7	2	3
7	1	2	8	3	5	4	9	6
2	7	6	3	9	8	5	4	1
8	9	4	5	1	2	3	6	7
1	5	3	4	7	6	2	8	9
4	8	1	6	5	3	9	7	2
9	6	7	1	2	4	8	3	5
3	2	5	7	8	9	6	1	4

18

6	7	9	5	4	2	8	3	1
1	2	4	8	3	9	7	6	5
8	3	5	6	7	1	4	2	9
2	4	1	3	9	7	6	5	8
5	9	8	1	2	6	3	7	4
7	6	3	4	8	5	1	9	2
4	5	2	7	1	3	9	8	6
9	8	7	2	6	4	5	1	3
3	1	6	9	5	8	2	4	7

19

8	4	7	9	5	1	3	6	2
5	6	1	3	2	8	9	7	4
3	2	9	4	7	6	1	8	5
6	3	2	7	8	5	4	1	9
7	8	4	1	3	9	5	2	6
9	1	5	2	6	4	7	3	8
1	9	3	6	4	2	8	5	7
2	7	8	5	9	3	6	4	1
4	5	6	8	1	7	2	9	3

20

1	7	2	3	8	4	6	9	5
4	5	9	1	2	6	8	3	7
3	6	8	5	7	9	4	1	2
8	1	4	7	5	3	2	6	9
6	9	5	2	4	8	3	7	1
7	2	3	9	6	1	5	8	4
5	3	1	6	9	2	7	4	8
9	8	7	4	3	5	1	2	6
2	4	6	8	1	7	9	5	3

Page 98

5	4	9	7	3	1	2	8	6						
6	7	8	9	2	5	3	1	4						
2	3	1	8	4	6	5	9	7						
7	9	2	5	1	4	6	3	8						
8	5	6	3	9	7	4	2	1						
4	1	3	2	6	8	9	7	5						
1	2	5	4	8	3	7	6	9	5	2	1	8	3	4
3	8	7	6	5	9	1	4	2	3	8	9	5	6	7
9	6	4	1	7	2	8	5	3	6	4	7	2	1	9
						5	2	7	8	1	3	4	9	6
						9	3	8	2	6	4	7	5	1
						6	1	4	9	7	5	3	2	8
						3	8	5	4	9	6	1	7	2
						2	7	6	1	3	8	9	4	5
						4	9	1	7	5	2	6	8	3

KJARPOSKO PUZZLES

This is how the test puzzle should look when it's finished:

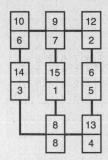

1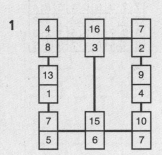

2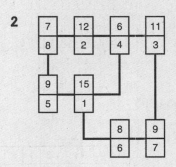

3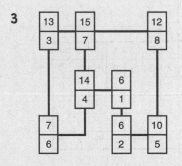

4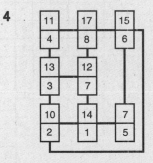

5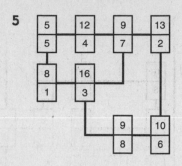

6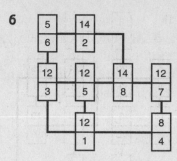

7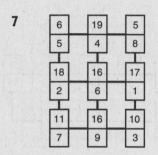

8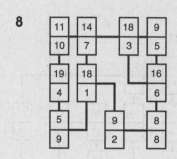

9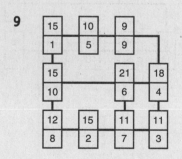

10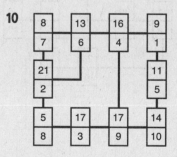

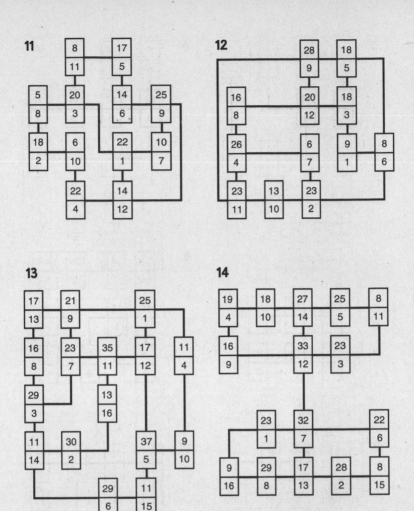

15

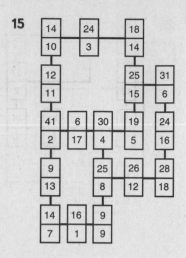

16

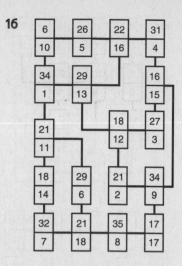

17

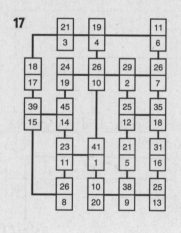

18

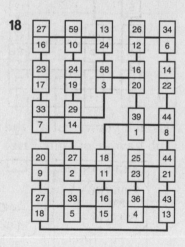

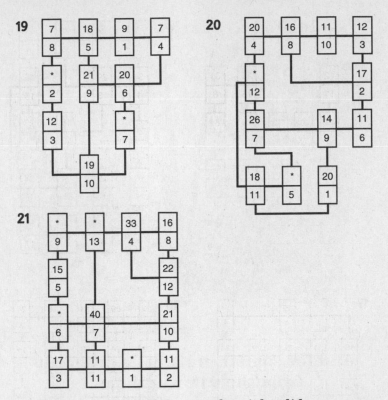

Even if you've got all the puzzles right, did you guess the flavour of your Prize Burger?

Addicted to puzzles? Try these!

0 439 95045 7   £2.99

Coming April 2006
0439 95000 7   £4.99

And for something a little different
from the same author...

0 439 96860 7   £5.99   0 439 95398 7   £5.99

.MURDEROUS MATHS.

Join the Murderous Maths gang for more fun, games
and tips at **www.murderousmaths.co.uk**